HOW TO BE REJUVENATED

IN LATER YEARS

OTHER BOOKS

HOW TO REGAIN AND RETAIN YOUR HEALTH AND YOUTH

Library of Congress Catalog Card # 88-91204

Printed in the U.S.A.

How To Be Rejuvenated In Later Years

Published by: Ida Alter
               Waltham Fl26, C.V.
               W. Palm Beach, FL 33417

ISBN #   0931113253

DEDICATION

This book is dedicated to oldsters like myself who want to get well, stay well, and are willing to get out of their chairs and do something about it.

I did it my way, even though my children in their concern yelled at me (for going holistic) and laughed at me (for using unorthodox methods) all the way until my leukemia went into remission.

A friend in my therapy group will not believe that I have no aches or pains. To be fit, full of pep and energy, you too, can overhaul your body simply, painlessly, and at no cost to you.

It is yours for the taking!

This is a book of Helpful Hints on how to feel better, look better, look more youthful, and live longer. It is not intended as a cure for any disease.

The author and publisher of this book disclaims any responsibility for any adverse effects resulting from the use of procedures outlined herein; and urge each reader to consult his or her personal physician before implementing any of these procedures.

This is the book all America is waiting for!

TABLE OF CONTENTS

Chapter   Page

i

CHAPTER ONE

HOW IT IS

This book starts where all other health books leave off. This is the book all America has been waiting for. Why? Because it's time for us to take responsibility for our own health. In this book I will tell you how to do it.

We are at this point now: We are living longer, but we are all sick. Government figures show that 92% of the American population is sick (Dr. Jensen, "Nature Has a Remedy"). And the doctors don't know what to do.

One doctor says, we don't know what steps to take to advance (Dr. James MacKenzie).

One health practitioner says, chronic fatigue is the scourge of the age (M. Carter).

One doctor said that he had to get away from the babblings of babbledom to understand where disease comes from (J.H. Tilden).

One doctor said, in the 22,000 surgeries I personally performed, I never saw one clean colon (H.M. Kellogg).

Another one says, the fighters, questioners, rebellious ones (patients) are the ones who get well (Dr. Bernard Siegel).

One doctor says, by the year 2,000 everyone will be taking tranquilizers (Dr. Kenneth F. Pelletier).

Oliver Wendell Holmes, M.D. once said, we should throw the whole materia medica to the bottom of the ocean.

Thomas Alva Edison said, the doctors of the future will give no medicine.

1

One doctor says we should all have been dead by 1970 (Dr. Levenson).

And the bottom line seems to be, "Only the body can cure itself" (Dr. J.H. Tilden).

A psychic forecaster says that we are on the threshold of the cure of diseases; but the answer will not be new. It may be surprisingly simple and come about through a "new way" of using something that has been at hand all along.

In this book, I will tell you the cause of disease, and I will tell you how to get rid of the cause. I will tell you how to cleanse the inside of your body in very simple, easy-to-do ways. You will feel good--full of pep and vitality; be healthier, look younger, possibly free of pain and disease, and have a longer lifespan, while at the same time listening to your doctor and following his advice.

This is a rejuvenation process. Would you expect your car to operate efficiently after 50, 60, 70 years without ever cleaning out the mechanism? Well, the body is the same--ignore it; keep piling more and more stuff into it than it can handle, and the result is more and more disease, sometimes even chronic, and this is where we are now.

Dr. John H. Tilden says there are no cures. You must remove the cause--the poisons in the body. Diet or food will not cure any disease. We must help nature eliminate the poisons.

We have at our disposal many ways to help nature eliminate the poisons in the body. I will tell you about these. The human body is an organized system that is self-adjusting, self-correcting, and self-improving--if that system is given new information. It wants to get well ("Body of Life", Thomas Hanna).

2

But—you have to do it yourself. Consider: Doctors are there for repairs and maintenance. The rest is up to us. We can have it either way, good health or otherwise.

Is it worth the trouble? Is it worth investing time and effort? Would you like to feel good into your 70's and 80's? It's up to you.

We are now in a situation where we accept functional disorders as inevitable, the effects of aging, or even unknown causes. But, we don't have to accept that.

Dr. Bernard Siegel ("Love, Medicine, and Miracles") says, "Our most successful patients are different in that they want to be in control. They drive doctors crazy, ask a lot of questions. Returning the power to the patient is funda-mental."

"In ancient China," says Felix Mann, MB. ("Acupuncture, The Ancient Chinese Art of Healing, and How it Works Scientifically"), "a first class physician was one who not only could cure disease, but could also prevent disease. Only a second class physician had to wait until his patients became ill so he could then treat them when there were obvious symptoms and signs. Their analogy in treating diseases that are already developed is like the behavior of persons who begin to dig a well after they become thirsty."

And that is what we have here. We wait until we get sick, can't see so well, can't hear so well, then go to the appropriate doctor for repair. And we must be thankful that they are there.

Everybody wants to feel good, stay young, live long; we don't want to age. But the way we

3

are living and the way we are eating is making the body degenerate and age.

If you don't do anything for the inside of your body, it will age in the normal way. But, if you want to hold back the aging process, you have it in your hands to do so.

How would you like to have a renewed body, to slow down the aging process, and—as a bonus—to remove facial wrinkles, bloated face, hanging eyelids, fat bellies! All this is possible with these simple methods. You do it yourself; it's inexpensive and painless. All you need is a little time and determination.

If you're sick, you're not up to par, you have a headache, you're slowing down, you're always tired and don't have enough energy, and the wrinkles are creeping up, and the doctor isn't helping you—what you need is a little self-help. It's easy. You'll never be uncomfortable. All you have to do is— Do it!

We've come a long way, Baby! But now we have to go back to see what we've been doing wrong.
We have to change to defensive living; we have to change to survive.

If you want to live longer, in good health; function well and have all the parts working well, dedicate yourself to cleansing. I will tell you how to do it. It's easy. All you need to do is to take that first little step.

Just consider: The miracle healer is the body itself!

So, as I've said, this book starts where all the other health books leave off. Here is where we get down to the nitty gritty. Here is a chance to do something wonderful for yourself.

4

Every day say to yourself, "What did I do nice for myself today?"

But wait--will you excuse me a minute? I have to go make a call. I'll be right back...

Chapter Two

A TALK WITH THE LORD

Me: Lord? Hello, Lord.

Lord: Yes?

Me: Lord, do you think we can have a talk?

Lord: Sure, any time. Come to me any time you want. That's what I'm here for.

Me: Lord, there's some things I'd like to ask you about, with your permission.

Lord: Sure.

Me: Lord, why are you making us all sick?

Lord: I was wondering when you would come to me about that.

Me: Yes, Lord. We're all sick down here. We're living longer, true, but we're all sick with all kinds of diseases; and there's no end. It's getting worse all the time. Do you know that people are getting sick at a younger and younger age?

Lord: You don't have to tell me. Don't you think I know what's going on down there?

Me: And me, too, Lord. I get these aches and pains all over all the time.

Lord: I know, I know.

Me: Lord, this is my life. I want to feel good, look good, enjoy life--and feel alive!

Lord: I know. I know you would like that, wouldn't you.

  Me: Lord, you bet. So what's wrong? Am I doing something wrong?

Lord: Well, you finally decided to come to me to find out. Do you really want to know?

  Me: Yes, yes, Lord. Tell me, please. Tell me what to do. I worked hard all my life; I just retired. Look, I love life--I just want to live a few more years and enjoy them in good health. That's not too much to ask, is it? Please tell me what to do. I'll do anything!

Lord: Okay. Sit down--no, sit over here where I can see you better. Listen; I will tell you. You know, when I first made the world, this is not what I had in mind--and as a matter of fact, sometimes I can't believe what I'm seeing. Is this what I made? Is this what I worked so hard for?

I don't say I made a perfect world, but it was as near perfect as it could ever be-- fresh healthy air, cool running spring water, a nice warm sun to make things grow, beautiful birds, animals, and everything well balanced so that none of them overrun the entire world.

But after I made the world, I was not satisfied. I felt that something was missing. It took many years before I figured out what it was. I finally figured out that what the world needed was Man.

So I worked on this about a million years and at long last I made one. I made a MAN!

7

What I put together was the most amazingly wonderful computerized body of a man-- so amazing that no one could ever duplicate a machine like that. Don't ask how much work I had to put into it. That was my best, though, and was I proud of it!

Consider: It has an electrical system, a food processor, plumbing, heating, and cooling systems. It is self-repairing and has a crew of paramedics who rush in the instant there is something wrong.

You probably don't know--the liver has over 500 jobs it must do. It knows when to do them and how to do them. The cells, blood, stomach--they all work automatically. I tell you; a machine like that cannot be duplicated anywhere.

It also has pressure points which are far removed from the organs and glands to help stimulate and repair them and bring them back to health. Ah, you're shaking your head. You didn't know about that.

Me: Yeah--you did pretty good.

Lord: Don't interrupt. Well, in the beginning, things went along alright. People had respect. They listened to me.

But now I can't believe what's going on. They have no respect at all for any-thing. And now, the way they abuse the body in every way they can----.

And they keep on doing this. It gets worse all the time; no respect for the body for years and years.

It hurts me plenty to see what's happening to it after all the thought and planning I

8

put into it. Do you think seeing the wrecks you all made of your bodies makes me feel good? With me, it's a matter of pride. I believed I had made such a beautiful thing.

Me: But Lord, I eat my bran every day.

Lord: Quiet; and listen. I gave them the most wonderful foods--so many herbs and even miracle foods. And every-thing is out there growing in the fields and on the mountains. But, people ignore them. That's what bothers me, too.

And, now you come to me and blame me for making you sick. No, my friend, you're bringing all these diseases on yourselves.

Me: Lord, I'm listening.

Lord: What I had in mind originally was responsible people, working the soil and leading a relaxed easy life--early to bed and early to rise--that sort of thing. But how do you live down there?

You're leading a fast life, at such a fast, frantic pace. It's like you're all rushing to extinction. Why, just turn on the TV and you'll see what I mean.

So, that's what's happening. You're killing yourselves on the inside. Aside from all that stress you get, tell me, what kind of food are you eating?

Me: Oh, the usual.

Lord: Now mind--I didn't put you all down there in a polluted world with 10,000 fast food restaurants for all you can eat (J. Winters). And with those sweet drinks...I

9

can't believe in some places those sweet
drinks are considered FOOD!

I'll tell you the truth, I have no patience
for all this nonsense. What are you all,
kindergarten children playing at living?

Listen, I'm God, the Lord of the
Universe...but a magician I'm not!

Me: I'm sorry, Lord. I didn't mean to upset
you.

Lord: I am upset. I'm angry and upset. You each
got a gift of a wonderful body. You don't
have to push a button to digest your food.
You don't have to push a button when you
have a BM. No, the body does everything
for you, automatically. You have so little
to do, and look what you've done.

It took a long time, but I knew sooner or
later you'd come running to me for help.

Me: I'm sorry, Lord. I'm sorry. Please tell
me what to do. I'll do anything. All I
want is just a few more years without any
sickness, to enjoy life a little bit
longer. Can you help me, please?

Lord: You don't deserve it.

Me: You mean you can make us all better if you
want? There's a way? You can do it?

Lord: I'll have to think about that. I'm not
sure you deserve any favors.

Me: Lord, please. I'll promise you anything.
Anything.

Lord: Okay. If you go out and spread the word, maybe they'll listen to you and then they'll all get better. You know it doesn't make me feel great to see what's going on down there.

Me: Then you'll tell me how? Please, please, Lord. I'll be forever grateful.

Lord: I don't know if I should tell you—you won't do it.

Me: I'll do it. I'll do anything, I promise. Lord, please, please, just tell me.

Lord: Well, it's really very simple. Go home and start cleansing the inside of your body. You'll be surprised with the results.

Me: That's it? That's the whole thing?

Lord: Yes. Actually, that's all that is necessary. Clean it out and you'll feel like a new person. You'll feel well and full of energy and vitality. No aches and pains. Your whole body will be renewed, energized.

Me: You mean that's all? That's the whole thing?

Lord: Yes. And I want you to spread the word. Tell everyone to do it.

Me: Oh, Lord, don't make me. They'll all laugh at me.

Lord: What do you mean?

Me: They'll never do it. You have no idea. Everyone is so sophisticated down there. We got yuppies, the rich and famous; we got VCR's, big cars, dyed hair, long polished

11

finger nails. Ha.   Who do you think is gonna go for this?

Lord: Well, wait a minute. Just wait a minute. It's really easy. All you have to do is take a tablespoon of this stuff with some seeds twice a day, and the job's half done. Now, is that so hard to do?

Me: No. They'll never do it.

Lord: If they give me back my pride I'll sweeten the pot. I'll throw in an extra bonus.

Me: What is that, Lord?

Lord: I'll help them get rid of fat.

Me: Well, maybe. They might just go for that. Thank you. Thank you, Lord. You make me feel so glad that I came to see you. Thank you and God bless you. Oh, what am I saying? You are God!

Lord: Go. Be on your way. Go and spread the word.

Me: Yes, yes. I'll do it. I'll try. I'll spread the word. I'll really try.

I LOVE LIFE!

CHAPTER THREE

WELLNESS

I said that this is the book all America is waiting for.

We have to realize what's happening here. We go along for years and years and years piling more and more stuff into our bodies than it can handle, and we get progressively worse on account of the poisons that are piling up and not being released, and what is the net result? The answer is degeneration and chronic disease.

In the Diamonds' book, "Fit for Life," they say, "Guess what's the one thing we don't do here in this country?" The answer is cleanse. It is said we don't have the mechanism here in this country to cleanse.

Then we start needing help for a myriad of diseases. We need all kinds of operations, heart, stomach, kidney, cataract; we need hearing aids, and we're given a little packet by the doctor to take home for a stool sample to check for blood in the colon--everything after the fact. We just wait till we get sick then we see to it.

But consider: NOTHING is done to prevent these things from happening! It's as if that's the normal process of aging. Can't we do anything to maintain good health ourselves? Is it possible for us to eliminate the poisons that cause these conditions?

Dr. N.W. Walker says that the human digestion processes were not intended to be called upon to convert these so called foods (white bread, biscuits, donuts, spaghetti, rice) into nourishment for the cells. These foods clog up the system resulting in such conditions as

13

arthritis, diabetes, coronary, varicose veins, hemorrhoids, kidney and gall stones.

Mrs. Carter (Reflexologist) says that the body becomes poisoned by our faulty lifestyle.

So what we're dealing with is poisons in the body. We are living at a frantic pace. This causes enervation; enervation causes stoppage of elimination of poisons; the poisons pile up and we have toxemia. Toxemia is the first, last and always the only cause of disease (Dr. J.H. Tilden).

What is actually meant by our frantic lifestyle? For instance do we ever rest to digest our food after a meal? Remember your working years when you ran an errand during your lunch hour, then bolted your food down, then went back to work? Who doesn't remember those days?

There was one popular restaurant in Manhattan, once the center of the garment trade industry, that had shelves for eating your lunch for those who were in a hurry.

Even today we have our food and then rush to our next appointment.

Any traveler through the European countries remembers that businesses were shut down for lunch and a siesta, then reopened in the late afternoon. But in this country, this is not our lifestyle.

So to deal with this problem of eliminating poisons, this is my program for regaining good health:

1.   The first and most important is a cleanse for the colon. This is where most of the body's problems start. If you're willing to open this Pandora's box and cleanse,

14

you'll be repaid a thousandfold in good health, vigor, vitality, youthful looks, and have a longer lifespan.

2. Another effective method of cleansing is through accupressure. This cleanses and stimulates the glands and organs. It is simple to do and certainly inexpensive. You do it yourself, with your own hands.

3. The next is the liver cleanse to improve the blood, which is the lifestream of the body.

4. The next cleanse is a fast. Stay with me. It need only be a one day a week fast, and I will tell you how to do it comfortably. When you see the benefits of this fast, you too will be anxious to do it.

5. Then we will learn about the miracle foods, of which there are many, and the wonderful things they do for the body.

So who says we have to age. By the use of all these methods of cleansing, and also by bolstering up your diet, you'll truly have a new lease on life, and your ego will swell from your improvement and from all the compliments you will be getting.

And it's easy. You can do it. All you have to do is decide to do it—to take that first step.

Are you dissatisfied with the way things are now? Tired of being tired? Dissatisfied with degenerating, with the aging process? Tired of seeing those wrinkles in the mirror? Then you're a likely candidate for this trip—a trip to the Garden of Good Health.

You need only a dedication to a renewal of yourself. Dr. Bernard Siegel ("Love, Medicine and Miracles"), says it's the fighters, the questioners, the rebellious ones who get well. This could be you.

What? You never did this before? You were never 70, 75 years old before!

CHAPTER FOUR

COLON

It has been a dream down through the ages of staying forever young; of prolonging the human lifespan, and man has searched for the Fountain of Youth all through history.

We travel the world over seeking elixirs, youth potions, herbs, cures. Movie stars and other prominent people visit the Hans Neiper Clinic in Europe to undergo rejuvenation treatments by cell implantation. Down through the ages the rich and powerful would give a king's ransom to be able to live longer. Can life be prolonged?

Dr. John H. Tilden says, "Medical science has not discovered why organs fail to function properly. But toxicity is the first, last and only cause of disease."

Jason Winters ("The Perfect Cleanse") says almost every chronic disease is directly or indirectly due to bacterial poisons absorbed from the intestines.

According to a British Medical Association, "Death begins in the colon," and there is much evidence that diseases originate in the colon.

The miracle healer is the colon cleanse. Don't go away. Listen a minute. You wake up in the morning feeling tired, sick, not up to par. You haven't any energy, you're slowing down, the wrinkles are creeping up on you. The doctor isn't helping you. You don't feel like getting out of bed.

How would you like to turn all that around? It's unbelievably simple. It's a self-help program. You can help yourself. Only you can do it. Just spend a half hour a day to feel great, look great, be full of pep and vitality. Sound good? It's yours for the taking. You can have it.

All that good health is right down there inside of you, and the body is willing, and even anxious, to cooperate with you. Give it a chance and it will go all out to heal itself.

You've had it your way up until now. You've had your steaks, roasts, fries, pies, and by this time, you need an overhaul. By cleansing, stimulating, and eating certain foods, you'll truly have a new lease on life. You like that? You'll get to live a few more years feeling good with no aches and pains.

It can be said that life and health begin in the colon! Most people's organs of elimination do not function well enough to handle all their waste, so the waste accumulates in the bloodstream and then the cells cannot utilize the fresh nutrients taken in by the body (Council of Nutritional Research).

Jason Winters searched the world over for the perfect cleanse, and he says, "I do know that rotting food and decaying fecal matter can be found in the colon that is at least five years old. It lodges in the pockets of the colon and just rots." He tells of a man's colon nine inches across with a passageway the width of a pencil for matter to pass through.

So now we understand that the killer is poisons in the body, and that is the cause of all diseases according to Dr. J.H. Tilden.

Diseases caused by toxemia are many:

Diseases of the stomach, liver, high blood pressure, weakened heart muscles,

arteriosclerosis, headache, pain in legs,
mental and physical depression, insomnia,
awakening tired, chronic fatigue, memory
loss, degenerated organs, changes in eyes,
hearing, wrinkles, muddy complexion,
arthritis, infection in bladder, kidneys—
the list is endless (Jason Winters).

What? You don't need it? You're clean
inside? Well, listen to Dr. Kellogg. We know of
Dr. Harvey Kellogg of Battle Creek, Michigan for
his breakfast cereals, mostly corn flakes. But
as a surgeon he said, "Of the 22,000 operations I
have personally performed, I have never found a
single normal colon." This was around the year
1900. Imagine what it must be today!

One man was found on autopsy to have
carried around with him forty pounds of fecal
matter in his colon. Can you imagine how he must
have felt, how slow his walk, how depleted his
energy, how colorless his face? And talk about
chronic fatigue or chronic diseases—or the aging
process! You have to look no further than the
colon.

How much better we would feel with a
cleansed colon! How many fewer trips we would
have to take to the doctor—doctors! How much
less medication we would have to take.
Medications are good when needed, but they have
side effects and taking too many medications can
cause more problems.

"In our culture we do not have the proper
techniques of cleansing the glands and the
cells." So says Dr. John Kelley, President of
the Council on Nutritional Research. His analogy
is, if we allow toxins to accumulate year after
year, the result would be far worse than if the
sewage and garbage collection in the City of New
York were to stop for twenty years! And we
wonder why we get sick!

19

But the good news is you can cleanse the colon simply, painlessly, inexpensively. (Or else have colonic irrigations done by a professional). But only you can make the choice. You just have to take the first little step. You've had it easy all these years, and—you need it NOW!

So—why not opt for a good, healthy cleansed body? Read on!

CHAPTER FIVE

A DREAM

One night after I did a colon cleanse, I went to sleep and had a dream. I dreamt my whole body was quiet and serene and in a beautiful place. At first I thought I was in heaven but there were no angels floating around. I didn't know why I felt so good. Every part of me was so relaxed; so in tune with every other part. And everybody around me was beautiful and healthy and smiling.

Suddenly, I heard the heart speak up. It was the first sound I heard in all the quiet. It said, "Hey, where is everybody? Get up, get up. Let's talk."

The liver was the first to speak up. "Here I am; it's me, the liver. Do you know the nice clean blood I'm getting down here now is fantastic. It's making my life so much easier. I really feel great, and I don't have to work so hard."

Then the lungs popped up. "Oh, I'm breathing. I'm breathing so good; no wonder we're all sleeping like babies."

Then the head: "Boy, is my head clear! Now I can remember things. I remember where I put my glasses. They're in the wrong drawer. And my book I searched all over the house for—it's up on the shelf. My head is so light, and everything is so clear!"

Then the eyes spoke up: "Hey, listen to me, everybody, listen to me. I can see. Wow! I can see so clearly. The blurry film is gone. I can't believe it. Boy, everything is so clear!"

Then the legs: "Look, look at this. I
have no more pain. And gee, I can walk, I can
walk! And I can bend my knee! Wait, let me see
if I can bend down to cut my toenails. Yea, I
can do it, I can! Gee whiz!"

The heart said, "Great! Now what about the
ears. Let's hear from the ears. Ears, Ears, are
you there?"

Ears: What?

Heart: Ears, I'm talking to you. Can you hear
me?

Ears: Oh, I'm sorry. I didn't hear you.

Heart: Why, are you having trouble hearing?

Ears: No, nothing like that. I was just
looking out the window watching a pretty
cell go by. What did you ask me? Oh
yes, I can hear fine. Just fine. No
complaint here.

Heart: Terrific. And how about you, Cells?

Cells: What? Who, me? I feel great.
Everything is moving along so fast just
like it used to when we were young.
Whee! Hey, who do I have to thank for
that?

Heart: For what?

Cells: Listen, Heart, let's not kid ourselves.
Somebody up there is doing a fantastic
job of cleansing; I can feel it. And
what a job that's doing on me! I'm
telling you I'm getting compliments from
all over--from everybody.

Heart: Like who?

22

Cells: Why just yesterday the eyes called me. You know all that trouble with the left eye, how blurred it was and all? Well, now she can even read the fine print, all the blurring cleared up.

Heart: You mean it?

Cells: Yeah. And I just can't believe what's going on down here. Will you please give my compliments to the boss when you see her. Oh yeah, and thank her especially for all that chlorophyll and all the sardines, too. I feel like a new person. Whee! I just feel like singing.

Heart: Go ahead. Don't let me stop you.

Cells: Great! Oh what a beautiful morning...la, la, la.

The brain was listening to all this and finally spoke up. "Guys, this is unbelievable. We finally got it all together. No more headaches, stomachaches, leg pains--everybody is feeling great.

"And say, wouldn't it be a good idea if the government opened up a colon clinic and everybody had to go there once a week for a free colon cleanse? Wouldn't that be great! What an idea! And how good everybody would feel! Everybody going for a colon cleanse every week. Boy, what an idea; I love it! We'll have to talk about that. Thank you all."

Heart: And now before we all go back to sleep, I think we ought to show our appreciation to the boss for being so nice to us, what do you say?

All: Great! I'll lower her cholesterol.

I'll lower her triglycerides.

I'll fix her blood count.

I'll see to her arthritis, her skin, memory—

Brain: Thank you, thank you, guys. Just what I wanted to hear. And you can be sure I will tell her how grateful you all are for her cleansing the colon for you. And now, back to sleep. Who's got the night shift?

When I woke up, I remembered vaguely the brain saying something like:

We don't have to accept aging as inevitable. The fighters can put it off for years and years in good health!

CHAPTER SIX

COLON CLEANSE

So now we come to the colon cleanse. Your doctor can't do it for you. Your doctor can help you when you have a specific problem but he can't give you a clean, healthy body. That's up to you. It's up to you to take that first little step.

Think of it. The entire medical profession is engaged in treating crises of toxemia, controlling it, and finally, we are victims of chronic disease (J.H. Tilden). But here we have long hidden secrets for good health right in our own hands.

The colon is a damp, dark place, ideal for breeding germs and bacteria. There are 36 different poisons that lodge in the colon.

As many people die each year from colon cancer as from auto accidents (University of California Berkeley Wellness Letter 7/85). And there is much suffering from polyps, ulcers, colitis, diverticulosis, hemorrhoids.

It may be said that almost every chronic disease known is directly or indirectly due to the influence of bacterial poisons absorbed from the intestines. The colon may be looked upon as a veritable Pandora's box out of which comes more human misery than from any other source (J. Winters).

Dr. Vanita Forsyth, who lost her colon to cancer surgery, has dedicated her life to treating others with colon problems and she has seen the following conditions either clear up completely or be greatly improved as soon as the person's bowel was cleansed:

25

Chronic fatigue, headaches, arthritis, high blood pressure, allergies, eye problems, constipation, leg cramps, hanging eyelids, bags under eyes, pot bellies, etc, etc.

With a cleansed colon, you can be forever young, look young, feel great, and be free of pain, and especially wrinkles. I'll settle for that!

And, it's so easy to do. So easy that you won't believe you can have all this with so little effort. Can you spare about half an hour a day? This is it:

Dr. Forsyth recommends Bentonite (which you can get at the health food store). It comes in powder form, in tablets, and in liquid form. I get the liquid. It's easier to take that way, and I find it more effective. All you have to do is take one tablespoonful in a glass of water in the morning and another in the evening. This can absorb 90 times its weight in toxins!

To this add a tablespoonful of psyllium seeds and drink the whole thing down. It is easy to take, and there is no taste or anything unpleasant to it. There, is that so hard to do?

Want to know what this does? There is layer upon layer of hardened fecal matter like a black rubber tire that is lining the colon. This mixture will soften and loosen up this hardened matter in the colon. The seeds swell up and become mucilaginous. I add a tablespoon of apple cider vinegar to it so I have the best of all worlds. And it's easy going down.

And the payoff? The payoff is a whole new lease on life! And now the fecal matter has been softened and loosened up. To wash it out, take an enema with water and apple cider vinegar (two tablespoonfuls to the bag). Keep the water in about 20 minutes while massaging the bowel area gently (Figure #1).

Fig. 1

I stay on this program for about a month, then stop and go back on after several months... with wonderful results!

However, you can't go on cleansing and cleansing. You must put some nutrients back. Beet tablets are recommended, and of course, your regular vitamins. I juice a beet in with carrot and celery juice, and sometimes an apple or fresh cranberries. It's a pleasant drink and so full of vitamins and minerals!

Of course, consult your own doctor about going on any of these programs, especially if you have a specific health problem. Total rejection

27

of orthodox methods of treatment or a doctor's advice is never recommended.

An interesting note about Jason Winters, author of "The Perfect Cleanse." As a daredevil, defying death, he travelled the world by balloon and canoe, he hunted polar bears, raced cars to test safety belts, crossed the Sahara by camel, and took death-defying risks as a Hollywood stunt man. But all those death-defying acts did not prepare him for the biggest test of all--facing death from terminal cancer. It is when disease strikes us that we become interested in our health and our bodies. Now he travels the world in search of more aids to good health.

So, do it--you'll feel great. Get rid of poisons and feel like a million! It's right there in your own hands!

CHAPTER SEVEN

WHAT IS DISEASE?

The medical world has been looking for a remedy to cure disease but nature needs no remedy. Nature needs only an opportunity to be able to heal itself.

Hippocrates said, "Natural forces within us are the true healers of disease." (Hey, I didn't know that.)

So what is disease? It is only the end result; the cause of disease is poisons in the body, and that is called toxemia. The only disease is toxemia, according to Dr. John H. Tilden.

The frantic pace of our lives slows down the elimination process, so the poisons stay inside the body and are not eliminated. Then the blood becomes charged with the poisons and this is toxemia, the cause of all diseases (J.H. Tilden).

After a time, deterioration sets in, but all diseases come from the poisons in the body. And every chronic disease starts with toxemia.

What does all this mean? It means that the way we live causes poisons to pile up in the body and the body can't eliminate them fast enough, and the end result is poisoning or toxemia, the first, last, and only cause of all so-called diseases (J.H. Tilden).

Western medicine has no sensible explanation. It can offer us no relief. Have you run the gamut of doctors; have you watched yourself age and felt trapped because your health

29

has not been like it used to be? Have you been told by your doctor, "You'll have to learn to live with it?"

Nature is its own miracle and will help you get well with a little bit of help, some effort on your part. But we don't know it. We might even ignore it if we knew. The healing cure is right there at your fingertips. You can do it yourself.

M. Carter (Reflexologist) says, "Nothing is incurable; diseases are the result of malfunctioning of body tissues due to unnatural elements of living."

Dr. Tilden says, "Afflictions or diseases cannot be 'cured.' Nature—our subconscious—has a full monopoly on the power to heal."

Jason Winters says cleansing the colon will alleviate chronic dragging abdominal pains, gastritis, distended abdomen (fat bellies) tenderness in the abdomen, as well as malfunctioning in many parts of the body.

Where do toxins come from? They come from two sources. The first is from the cells splitting. Half the cells stay in the body and rebuild, and half of the cells die and have to be eliminated. If they are not removed fast enough, this causes poisons in the body.

The second source of poisons is from undigested food, of which cooked, fried, sauteed, barbecued, and processed foods are contributing factors.

And if the power to digest is not increased, says Dr. Shelton, all attempts to build up the body will be useless. (There is a natural aid to undigested food in the body. It's bee pollen, one of nature's miracle foods. This

30

helps to eliminate the undigested food in the body. It is available in health food stores.)

So, now are you ready for the colon cleanse? Your doctor can't do it for you. Your doctor can help you when you have a specific problem, but he can't give you a clean, healthy body. That's up to you. Only you can do it.

It is not easy for us to realize that 35 million years ago man was made to eat raw foods. We cannot conceive of such a world. But one day I imagined that I was there 35 million years ago, and this little scene is what I saw.

CHAPTER EIGHT

CAVE BEARS
(With apologies to Jean Auel)

It is some 35 million years BC. The people are living in huts made of buffalo skins, and it is so cold, with the north wind blowing through the hut, that the little old woman couldn't take her polar bear dress off all winter.

There is no language; but the people have their own system of communicating either by a grunt, of which they had a fairly complete vocabulary, or by a wave of the hand.

Nakomowitz is sitting in the warmest corner of the tepee and talking to her husband, Sitting Bullvon, also known as Sam. But hunger is hunger anywhere, and there is nothing for her to serve her husband for supper, not even an old salami. So she grunted, "Harrumph." That meant, Sam, run down to the supermarket and get something for supper.

"Blosk," grunted Sitting Bullvon. That meant, What should I get?

"Brushek:" How about some fried chicken?

"Whoosk:" What part should I get—breast or drumstick? grunted Sam.

"Brumph:" Birdbrain, use your judgement.

"Whoosky," grunted Sam.

"Ladj:" What did you say?

"Whoosky," repeated Sam.

"Midge," grunted Nakomowitz. Okay, get a half pound of cole slaw and some potato knishes... Maybe a sour pickle or two.

"Harrumph," Sam grunted again.

"Narrumph:" Listen, blubber, grunted Nakomowitz, you're fat enough. You don't need any jelly donuts.

"Haldaj," said Sam.

"Golidaj:" No. No chocolate cookies either, fat face. But I'll make you a nice cup of padjky.

"Padjky, nadjky," grunted Sam. Your darn padjky is making me crazy. I was up all last night warping from your padjky.

(At this Sam began to spit, and it froze in his beard.)

"Aboulajah," grunted Nako. God, look at you; I can't bear to look at you any more. Why don't you get a shave and a haircut while you're in town.

"Waboosa:" Alright, I'll go. Stop nagging, already.

"Brimba," grunted Nako. And tell him to cut it real short. Every time you get a haircut you need another one in 30 moons.

"Babool:" Okay, okay, already. Stop with your nagging. Listen, get me an alcha seltzer, will you. That darn potato kugel with all that pepper you gave me yesterday is sticking me right here. You're giving me indigestion with your cooking.

"Hazoon," grunted Nakomowitz. Boy, are you nuts. You stuff yourself and stuff yourself and then you complain to me.

"Blablock:" It's you, grunted Sam. You're ruining my stomach. Listen, go next door and see if Mrs. Goldberg has an alcha seltzer.

"Balooz:" Bullvon, you're out of your mind. Don't you know she doesn't believe in that stuff? How many times do I have to tell you--she doesn't need alcha seltzers. She eats these berries from the bushes and makes broccoli ice cream and cookies...And she reads Preventive magazine.

"Hapoch," grunted Sam. Do you mean to say— are you telling me she never goes to the doctor? She never stepped foot in a hospital?

"Gratch:" Negative.

"Hapoch," said Sam. What? Does she pay for Medicare and Blue Cross for nothing?

"Blotch," said Nako. You got it.

"Hadjek:" Hmmmm.

"Maldik," said Nakomowitz. Believe. Believe what I'm telling you.

"Hochik," said Bullvon. Okay, okay. Listen, give me the shopping list. Better write everything down and let me get going.

"Balchik," grunted Nakomowitz. Oh, and get me a bottle of Bylonol, extra strength, while you're there. My arthritis is acting up again. What's holding you up?

"Blabbish," grunted Sam. Oh, hell. I can't get the car started. Hey, woman, run next door

and see if you can borrow a cup of blobl, and
hurry up, will you, my hands are freezing.

"Noblish:" And yeah, grunted Sam, get me the
fleishedick tomahawk. Maybe I can catch a
buffalo on the way back. I'm dying for a nice
hot buffaloburger with all the trimmings. Hey,
have we got some of that cheese to go with it?

"Gimlitz:" Is that all you got on your mind?
Food? grunted Nako. Go already.

Nakomowitz waved. There was no word for Get
Lost.

CHAPTER NINE

ENDOCRINE GLANDS

Don't let the term endocrine glands scare you. They are the life force. They influence our health, our looks, happiness, and our way of life. You are either keen or dull, quick or slow. You have immunity, drive, energy, are animated, or depressed. The glands send energy all through the body.

Over the years, the body slows down and the glands become sluggish, and the whole picture is one of aging. Stimulating the flow of fresh blood to these places brings new life to the glands and retards the aging process.

Reflexology is a process of cleansing and stimulating the glands. You will be delighted at the ease with which this is done; only you must not go at it too vigorously at first because the body will release too many toxins at the same time, and it will not be able to handle them all at once.

Before you get out of bed in the morning (and at any time of the day) you can give yourself this pep-up treatment for the glands and you'll jump out of bed full of vigor and vitality and raring to go. Within minutes you will get a burst of energy from opening up the blocked and sluggish areas through the body.

The method: There are several areas in the hands to press and massage. This will stimulate the entire system of glands and send vital life force through your body. Does it sound easy? It is. Do this 2 to 3 minutes every other day the first two weeks. This is absolutely harmless and has no side effects.   See Fig.#2.

1.   The Spleen--This is a storage container of life energy force. Massage below the little finger of the left hand only.

2 and 2A. The pituitary and pineal glands located in the center and side of pad of thumb. The pituitary gland is the king gland. Apply pressure and hold 15 seconds.

The pineal gland is on the side of the thumb. This sets the tone for all the glands. Apply pressure by squeezing the sides of the thumb.

3.   The area in the center of the palm is the pressure point for three glands:

a)Thymus: This influences immunity to disease.
b) Pancreas: Watches the sugar level.
c) Adrenal gland: For keenness, drive, energy, vigor, and perception.
Massage this area.

4.   The Thyroid--On the thick pad below the thumb. This is the iodine depot. You are either dull or alert, quick or slow, animated or depressed, depending on the activity of the thyroid. Massage this area.

4A.   The Parathyroid--Alongside this pad. This controls metabolic function (metabolism is vital in eliminating toxins. This is what we've been talking about--removing waste).

5.   Gonads, Sex Glands--This is what gives the body flexibility, a sparkle in your eye, and personal magnetism. This gland is located 2 to 5 inches up from the wrist on the outside of the hand. Massage this gland by placing the thumb of the other hand on top of your hand and the forefinger

on the under side of your hand and caterpillar your way up for several inches.

A few minutes' workout on these glands every morning before you get out of bed and you'll be charged up like a new battery and raring to go. It is amazing that in a few short minutes, you can be full of pep and electrical energy and ready to face the new day with renewed vigor and vitality.

This chapter deals only with the pressure points to the glands. We will talk about the pressure points relating to the organs of the body in a later chapter. But here you have a good start for the day.

We DO have the power to get well and stay well, right there at our fingertips!

Figure 2

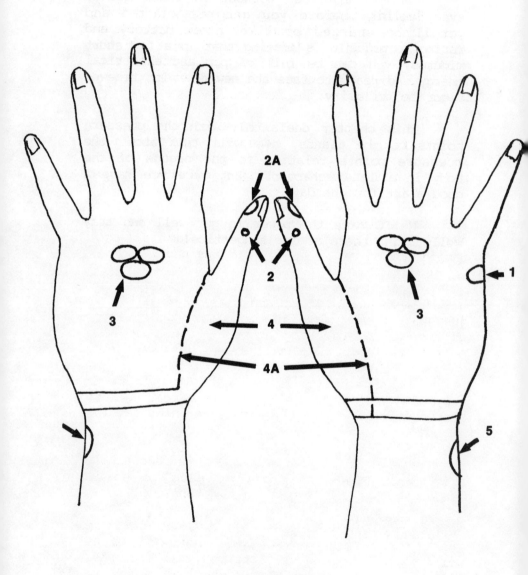

Endocrine Glands

39

CHAPTER TEN

THINK POSITIVE

Healing today is big business, and it's gotten to be a large percentage of our GNP (Gross National Product). It's a large part of the economy. I'm not sure I feel comfortable with the idea that I'm boosting the GNP every time I go to the doctor or the hospital.

We have many and bigger hospitals, big doctor bills, a very successful pharmaceutical industry, radiologist bills, pathology, x-ray bills, and more and bigger nursing homes. Business is good.

Dr. Sidney Wolfe, one of Ralph Nader's Raiders, says that the National Institute of Health should be in the banking business.

Isn't there any way we can control our health? Is health a hit and miss process? Do we just have to rely on luck to be in good health, or can we do something about it? Can we have some control over our health?

The answer is a great big YES! We can do many things for ourselves to feel good and to resist disease. All you need is an understanding of the body and a desire to help yourself.

We can be our own doctor. This is entirely within our capability; all we need to do is decide to take matters in our own hands.

Actually, your mind has a great part in getting and staying well. Do you want to be well? Nobody will give it to you. It's simple. All you have to do is think well! Think you're going to survive. Think you're going to be fit, full of energy like you once were, and think yourself beautiful.

A few years ago when I sick and looking poorly, a little friend of mine said I was beautiful. How she could say that I could never figure out, but when I looked in the mirror I saw myself as beautiful, and I try to keep telling myself this ever since.

So, we can think ourselves well; think ourselves looking better.

I have a friend, Estelle, who is 80 years old. She is thin, has a beautiful complexion, and she still tap dances. She hasn't seen a doctor in twenty years. She says, "My food is my doctor."

A neighbor of mine was asked by her doctor what she does to keep looking so young. When I asked her the same thing the other day she said, "Walking is my doctor."

One lady I know told me she rests at home one day a week, and has been for the last 60 years. (She is past 80.) That's her doctor.

One lady who is pushing 80 told me that her mother took a glassful of water enema every morning for forty years. Her mother died at 96.

I say the enema is my doctor. That keeps you feeling good and feeling young. So, let's get rid of the accumulated poisons in there and get back to health. I think THAT is a wonderful doctor.

We can help ourselves to better health, and by doing so find that we need less medication and be better off for it.

Dr. Joseph M. Scavone (Tufts University School of Medicine, Medford, Massachusetts), says that, "we are likely to need, and use, a greater variety of medications as we age" (Future Youth).

41

Are we to assume that aging is a disease?
I don't think so. But the longer we live in our
present lifestyle, the more poisons we will have
accumulated in the body, and this is what causes
disease.

What was that the doctor said? "You'll
have to learn to live with it." Not if you
believe what the doctors (in this book) and other
health practitioners are saying!

Visual imagery is becoming more and more
popular. See yourself well. Think yourself
well. Think positive. You can get well and stay
well.

Dr. Irving Ooyle says, "The mind controls
the body, and we can perhaps get well by learning
to control our bodies" ("The Foot Book,"
Berkson). That's what Dr. Carl Simonton says.
That's what Dr. Norman Cousins says also.

Think about that and take control of your
own health. No one can do it for you. You have
to do it yourself.

Go to it! And think positive!

CHAPTER ELEVEN

REFLEXOLOGY

Dr. Ross Trattler in his book, "Better Health Through Natural Healing," says that the body is equipped with sophisticated defense mechanisms designed to protect itself from a reasonable threat. (All together now,—"I didn't know that!")

"It can clean itself of unneeded or unwanted or toxic substances provided channels are not blocked. When vital force is suppressed, disease sets in." So with reflexology, we have a good way to accomplish this—just keep the channels open and unobstructed.

This is our present situation:

1. The body is clogged up with poisons from our life style and from the way we eat.

2. The doctors are baffled because they can't make us well, and we get sicker and sicker starting at an earlier age as time progresses.

3. We have many natural methods of helping ourselves to get well and stay well and reflexology is one of them.

Devaki Berkson, reflexologist and author of "The Foot Book," says she had been ill for a long time in her earlier years. She had seen doctors and had undergone operations and all this left her in misery, even bewilderment, and she felt like no one knew what to do, or even cared.

She stumbled into the hands of a foot reflexologist, and with regular treatments, diet and an exercise program, her problems lessened, and finally disappeared, which made her decide to study the art of reflexology and to go on to treat others.

What is reflexology? There are points in the hands and feet that reach every part of the body. By applying pressure to these points it releases blockage, poisons, and accumulated wastes, and these are eliminated through the liver and kidneys.

Eureka! Another method of cleansing the body, simply and easily. The psychic said that we had a simple method all along, and there it is. What could be simpler than applying pressure with our fingertips.

So give nature a chance to put your body chemistry back--a chance for natural healing; no doctors, no medications!

What will reflexology (or acupressure) do for you?

1. Step up the blood supply.
2. Stimulate gland function.
3. Stimulate the organs.
4. Release waste products.
5. Give you pep and energy.

While massaging, when you find a tender spot, massage it a few minutes to release a flow of electrical life force into the congested area. Then leave the spot and return to it later. Mrs. Carter says, "If it hurts, rub it out."

Mrs. Carter says that you can get relief from practically all your aches and pains, and also help heal chronic cases that have not yielded through other methods of treatment.

But start with two or three minutes on each hand every other day at first so that the body doesn't release more poisons than it can handle

at once. After about two weeks, you can do this
every day.   (See Fig.#3).

So—keep yourself in good health. Massage
the reflexes!

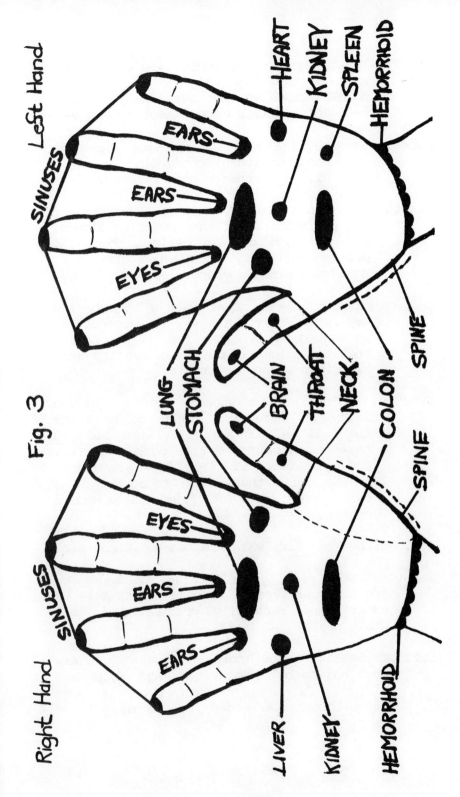

Fig. 3

Left Hand

Right Hand

HEART
KIDNEY
SPLEEN
HEMORRHOID
SINUSES
EARS
EARS
EYES
SPINE
LUNG
STOMACH
BRAIN
THROAT
NECK
COLON
SPINE
EYES
EARS
EARS
SINUSES
LIVER
KIDNEY
HEMORRHOID

45A

CHAPTER TWELVE

THE CASE OF THE ADORABLE
COL. OLIVER NORTHEAST

Scene: Senate Hearing Commission Senator Inouihaha, Chairman, conducting.
Col. Oliver Northeast on the stand.

Senator Inouihaha: Col. Northeast, I understand you're in charge of the endocrine glands, and you made certain deals without the proper authority of elected officials. Would you explain your role?

Col. Northeast: Well, that wasn't exactly the way it was, sir. The way it happened was we wanted to save the abdulla oblongata, and it was agreed that this was the most expedient way to do it sir.

Senator: Colonel, under whose authority did you sell the endocrine gland and to whom? And tell us, if you will, whom did you have to account to? Speak up, sir. Don't be bashful. You know you got a pretty smile there, and those big blue eyes don't detract from the picture either.

Col. Northeast: Sir, what was the question, sir?

Senator: Now, don't get flustered, Colonel. We are all your friends up here. Just tell us under whose authority you acted in all those deals.

Col. Northeast: No authority, sir. We just saw what had to be done, and we went ahead and did it. No sir, no authority, sir. We never thought we needed it. No sir!

Senator: Tell us, Colonel, did the President
           know? What did the President know about
           this, and when did he know it?

Col. Northeast: Oh no, sir. The boss never knew
           anything about this. Oh no. Whenever we
           would meet we all just sat around and
           laughed and joked. He told us how he made
           movies and the one where he lost his legs.
           That was his favorite one. He told us he
           asks Nancy to check his legs every night to
           make sure they're there. Did we laugh! We
           loved that one. What was the question,
           sir?

Senator: Did the President know anything about
           your dealings?

Col. Northeast: Oh no, no sir. We never told
           the boss anything. That's how we were able
           to go ahead with the metabolism deal.
           Yeah.

Senator: Tell us, Oliver, and would you please
           look me straight in the eye. Right at me,
           that's it. Tell me, did there ever come a
           time when you actually sold off the
           metabolism? When was that, and to whom?

Col. Northeast: Well, we first started by
           selling off the metabolism in exchange for
           papahydropen, and next we exchanged some
           for hogibogenfen, and before you know it, I
           was getting a little worried so they put an
           electronic security blanket around my desk.
           Yeah. But I gotta tell you, sir, we were
           doing fine. Really. We had this great big
           Swiss bank account and all.

Senator: I didn't ask you about that yet, Ollie.
           But tell us what happened next. Please

feel free and at ease. We are all with
you, you know. Tell us what happened after
that.

Col. Northeast: Well, sir, we were doing fine.
Like I said, we had this great Swiss bank
account going and everybody was having fun
and laughing, when one day the attorney
general, what's his name, came by, and we
had a great party. We ordered up some
roast beef and stuff and we were having fun
and telling jokes. But then we had enough
partying, sir, and I went back into my
office; yes, in the next room, and shredded
up all the rest of the roast beef and
stuff.

Senator: Sounds like fun, Ollie. Go ahead,
please.

Col. Northeast: Yes, sir, was it ever. Oh, and
Fawn, my secretary. You shoulda seen her.
She had on this cute little mini skirt, and
her hair was all up in a pony tail, cute as
a button, I tell you.
But she's not just another pretty face.
She kept on the job all during her lunch
hour, shredding and shredding till
everything was all done and gone, and then
the attorney general, what's his name, was
allowed to come in.

And, oh yeah, I can't wait for Fawn's book
to come out, and the movie and all, sir.

Senator: Tell us, Ollie, why did you shred all
the shredding?

Col. Northeast: Well, Senator, sir, we didn't
want to get caught with our endocrines
down, you know how it is.

Senator: Yes, sure, Ollie. That sounds cool.
And now, Ollie, will you tell us, if you
don't mind, what ever happened to all the
toxins. There were 20 million toxins
unaccounted for that passed hands in the
deal. Where is all that, Oll?

Col. Northeast: Oh, I don't know, sir. I sure
don't.

Senator: Are you telling us that 20 million
toxins can be flushed down the john just
like that?

Col. Northeast: Oh, I don't know, sir. I wish I
knew so I could tell you. Really!

Senator: Oh, those big blue eyes, Ollie; they
look so honest! Can you just turn to the
side, can you Ollie, so the cameras can get
a better view. Wow! And now, Ollie, can
you tell us any more?

Col. Northeast: Well, Senator, I sure wish I
could remember, sir. Some of it, I think--
let's see, I think 10 million of it we gave
away. Oh yeah, to General Shakeum-up, if I
remember correctly, and frankly about the
other 10 million gee, I'm afraid I'm a
little fuzzy about that. It's possible
that we put that away somewhere in a Swiss
bank, too. Gee!

Senator: Are you telling me, Blue Eyes, that we
have ten million in a Swiss account? That
stuff belongs to the government you know,
Ollie.

Col. Northeast: Yes sir. I know, sir. I wish I
could help you, sir. But we lost the
number of the account.

49

Senator: You lost the number of the bank
account? Hahaha. Hey fellas, they lost the
number of the Swiss bank account. (They
huddle.) Hahaha. Well, that's okay,
Ollie. Think nothing of it. There's
plenty more where that came from. Don't
you worry about a thing.

Col. Northeast: Thank you, sir. Thank you.

Senator: Now, can you tell us, Oll, I mean, tell
us one more time, under whose orders were
you working?

Col. Northeast: Well, sir, it all started in the
basement, and then the media got hold of
it. The media is connected to the thigh
bone and the thigh bone is connected to the
medulla, and before we knew it, we were on
a roll.

Senator: I understand perfectly, my boy. Tell
me, Oll, did the President ever know about
this, and when did he know it?

Col. Northeast: Oh no, sir. We did have a
couple of fun meetings with the boss, and
when we got to the good parts, he always
fell asleep.

But anyway, he told us he couldn't care
less about the metabolism and all that
stuff, sir. All he had on his mind were
his polyps. He always carried a little box
of Preparation H with him.

Senator: I see, I see. Well, if there are no
further questions from the panel, I would
like to close this hearing. Ollie, you did
a wonderful job of protecting the
metabolism and disposing of all the
toxins... and let's forget about the bank
account number. No matter.

And now the panel and I wish to thank you for bothering to come down here and tell us everything we wanted to know. We all appreciate your giving up your valuable time to come down here and telling us what we wanted to know, don't we boys?

Col. Northeast: My pleasure, sir.

Senator: And now, to show you our appreciation, we have some nice surprises for you. First, we want to present you with the Congressional Medal of Honor for truth-telling and for the fine job you have done. But, that's not enough to show you how we feel. We also have for you a Boy Scout Honor Badge dipped in gold. Wear it proudly. Also, we have for you two weeks' vacation, for you and Fawn, at the Hawaii Hilton. Go, enjoy!

Col. Northeast: Oh, thank you, sir. Thank you.

Senator: And wait. There's more. We also have for you a great big movie contract for 23 billion dollars for one year with a 5 year escalating clause. Who knows where this could escalate to. The movie industry sure appreciates an honest face. And finally, I just want to say thank you for sharing all this with us. It's been so much fun, hahaha. And look; we don't give a damn if the president knew, or when he knew, right boys? So long, Ollie.

Oh, what fun! I wish all our days were like this!

CHAPTER THIRTEEN

COFFEE

The coffee enema is my #3 method for cleansing. This cleanses the liver. If you don't like the gray or yellow color of your complexion, here is a treat for you.

If you want to get well, have energy, vitality, feel young, and look young, here is a natural, simple, inexpensive, and wonderful way to get there. Here's nature's way--you don't need medications.

One lady was shocked at the idea of taking an enema, and a coffee enema at that. She said, "Do I have to take the enema?" I said, "Pretend that a cancer doctor told you do to it." There were no further questions.

Many doctors recommend the coffee enema. Dr. Vanita Forsyth, who is dedicating her practice to the cure of cancer of the colon, says that within minutes the coffee enema can alleviate headache, leg cramps, aches and pains, feverishness, and many other symptoms.

Dr. John W. Kelley (President of Council on Nutritional Research) recommends the coffee enema, even as many as three or four times a day when necessary.

Dr. Jensen ("Nature Has a Remedy") says that Dr. Max Gerson, known the world over for his research and treatment of cancer, would have his patients set their alarm clocks to get up in the middle of the night when toxins are released, to take coffee enemas. They would take two or three a night to get rid of toxic waste that the body was breaking down and throwing into the colon. He made sure the toxic waste was eliminated consistently.

What does the coffee enema do? It pulls out a toxic reaction in minutes. And just letting in the coffee and retaining it stimulates the bowel walls, and the bowel will rid itself of some of the putrid matter. You must also use a gentle massage says Dr. Forsyth.

To two cups of boiling distilled water add 3 heaping tablespoons of regular ground coffee (not decaf) and let it boil about 3 minutes, then let simmer for 10 minutes and cool to room temperature. Then add two tablespoonsful of blackstrap molasses.

Pour into a plastic see-through enema bag (Fleet enema bags sold in drug stores for less than $3). When ready, lie on the left side and insert the tube in the colon about 18 inches. Suspend enema bag not more than 20 inches above area. Placing it higher will allow the coffee to go in too fast, and you will not be able to retain it. Leave the coffee in for 20 minutes, massaging the colon area. Lie on the left side 5 minutes, then on the back for five minutes, then on the right side for 5 minutes.

Between cleansing the glands, the colon, and the liver, you can't imagine how good you will feel. You will feel like a new, younger person. You will feel like running and jumping. An added bonus is the psychological effect that makes you feel so good knowing you're doing something wonderful for yourself.

Besides feeling and looking better, your self esteem will soar—boost your ego. Look at this remarkable thing you're doing for yourself— giving yourself a whole rejuvenation treatment. You'll love yourself for it. And you, too, will feel that the coffee enema is a miracle.

CHAPTER FOURTEEN

FASTING / RESTING

We now understand that toxins (poisons) are the basic cause of all diseases. Rest and sleep help get rid of poisons and are necessary for a sufficient supply of energy.

We are told that we have the power to heal ourselves, that the body is self-adjusting, self-correcting, and self-improving, and all we have to do is tell it what to do. It has a built-in bias toward effectiveness ("Body of Life," T. Hanna).

But our hectic lifestyle doesn't allow for much rest. However, the superior way to relieve toxemia is by fasting and resting. Dr. Herbert Shelton says there is no better way to release poisons than by fasting.

Think of it: the entire medical profession is engaged in treating us—and in the end we have chronic diseases. But here we have at hand so many simple secrets for good health! Amazing!

What does fasting do? It gives the body a chance to help itself. Healing proceeds at an accelerated rate during a fast. The body will choose to break down and burn first the material which is hampering normal functioning. When a person fasts, the body's healing powers are at no time more active (Science Health, Nov/Dec 1982).

Dr. Shelton says, "Physiological rest (fasting)—rests the over-worked digestive system. All organs of the body reduce their activity and the body is able to free itself of accumulated toxic waste. Needed also are water and sleep."

Fasting has got to make you feel good and help build healthy cells and tissues in the body. It has got to give you energy, vitality. And you get a plus for your ego for doing another wonderful thing for yourself.

Besides, isn't this what we were supposed to do? Wasn't this preordained? Didn't the Bible say to work six days and rest on the seventh? There it is, the original design. But you can ask your doctor whether you can do this.

You may be surprised to learn that Russia has free government sponsored fasting centers (Devaki Berkson).

Also, sleep speeds healing, speeds tissue renewal. Cell division is fastest and immune system is most efficient. It aids memory, too.

I like to fast one day a week, drinking water, a little juice, and some clear soup. That makes it very pleasant, and I find myself looking forward to my next day of fasting.

I do that one day a week; you have to stay in bed and keep warm. I find that after several weeks on this program that I have more and more energy.

For a longer period of fasting, it is recommended that this be done under supervision and ideally away from home where it is more conducive to staying on this program.

Devaki Berkson says to fast on vegetable juices once a week, especially beets, carrots, and apples mixed together.

Okay. Try it. You'll like it!

CHAPTER FIFTEEN

WATER

We all know that without water, we can't live. And the kidneys can't function properly without enough water.

Water helps rid the body of waste. There it is again, another way to release toxins. You can release toxins by drinking water.

But what happens when the kidneys don't get enough water? Three things happen:

1.   The kidneys store water in the hands and feet, causing swelling.

2.   It steals water from the colon.

3.   Since it can't function adequately without sufficient water, it dumps some problems on the liver.

And so we are left with:

1.   Swollen ankles or legs or hands.

2.   Dried fecal matter in the colon.

3.   A liver that can't do its job of getting rid of fat. So—you put on weight.

And all because you didn't give it enough water.

Why does the kidney store water in the hands and feet? When it gets insufficient water, it sees this as a threat of a drought, so it starts hoarding every drop it can—in the legs, ankles, and hands. And you say, "Oh gee, my leg is swollen. I wonder what that's from."

When the body does get enough water, it will release the water it's been storing in the swelling. It works like a finely tuned piece of machinery.

When the kidney takes water from the colon, it leaves the colon dried out and there's a formation of layer upon layer of dried fecal matter in the colon. This turns black and hard as a rubber tire. And the result? Diseases, deterioration of the body and...aging.

So, believe it or not, to get rid of excess weight, drink more water. How simple, easy, inexpensive. So, again, what does sufficient water do:

1. Helps the body get rid of poisons.
2. Gets rid of swelling.
3. Gets rid of fat.
4. Purifies the cells.
5. Plumps up the skin.
6. And what a marvelous bonus—you'll lose weight!

Dr. Shelton says to drink only pure water. The public water supply in most of the U.S. is not fit for human consumption.

The kidney must strain impure water, and it must work day and night. If the kidneys fail to strain the impurities out, you see the effects all through your body—thickened joints, painful nerves, weakened arteries, rheumatism, various disturbances of circulation (Council on Nutritional Research).

So, try it. Try drinking more water. You'll love the way you'll feel. And if you're with me up to now, you've got to be feeling like a million dollars. "The Snowbird Diet," Donald S. Robertson, Warner Books Magazine.

CHAPTER SIXTEEN

DRAGNET
(With apologies to Jack Webb)

Tum ta tumm tumm.

It's 7:02 A.M. The morning is fine. The air is clear. The Heart and Assistant knock on the door.

Heart: We want to see the Kidney.

Kidney: I'm the Kidney.

Heart: Your Medicare card, please.

Kidney: Why? What'd I do?

Heart: There's an APB out on you.

Kidney: I ain't done nothing.

Heart: There's swelling on the left ankle.

Kidney: I didn't do it.

Heart: We want the facts. Just the facts.

Kidney: Well, gee, I had to save some water for my wife and kids.

Heart: A confession. Take that down, George.

Kidney: How do I know if there's gonna be a shortage?

Heart: Just the facts, sir.

It's 7:05 A.M. The sky is clouding up.

Kidney: Hey, know what happened to me the other day? The boss went for a hike in the woods. I didn't see a drop of water all day.

Heart: You got that, George?

Kidney: Gee, what am I saying? Even when the boss is home and water is near, he still doesn't give me any.

It's 7:23 A.M. It's drizzling outside.

Heart: You're stealing from the colon.

Kidney: What if I borrowed a cupful from the colon? You call that stealing?

Heart: George, read him his rights.

Kidney: I'm innocent--innocent I tell you!

Heart: Now we got him on a 703.

Kidney: No, no. I just took a cupful. I swear it.

Heart: George, put the cuffs on.

Kidney: No, no, leave me alone.

Heart: Now we got him on a 504. Resisting an officer.

Tum ta tum tumm.

It's 7:30 A.M. The sky is over-shadowed. It's starting to snow.

Heart: And you've been dumping on the liver. Just the facts, sir.

Kidney: It's all on account of the boss. If he would only give me my 8 glasses of water in the first place, I wouldn't have to go sneaking around stealing and stashing and dumping.

Heart: Full confession. Got that, George? Better take him downtown.

Kidney: Hey, wait, wait. I need to have a drink now, please. Please. My throat is parched, too. I'm dying. Help me, help me.

Tum ta dum dumm.

It's 7:32 A.M. The siren is screaming as they speed through the streets.

CHAPTER SEVENTEEN

LOUISIANA STATE PRISON

Scene: Louisiana State Prison

Action: Riot--1987

Kidney: Hey, hello--hey, you there. Warden. Listen, jerk. This is the Kidney in Cell Block 13. Yeah, I'm out of the cell. Where the hell you think I'm calling from?

Warden: Get back in your cell.

Kidney: Come off it, crumb. I got three hostages.

Warden: Get back in your cell, I said. Where's the guard? Who you holding hostage?

Kidney: Yeah, I got the stomach, liver, and bladder. And hey, we got knives.

Warden: I see smoke coming out. You set fire, too?

Kidney: Yeah, you're getting on to it. Hey, get this and get it quick. Me and the hostages are in a hurry, so stop p--- around.

Warden: Okay, okay, cool down and get back in your cell. I don't want no riot here.

Kidney: Bull. If we don't get what we want, we're blowing up the joint.

Warden: What the hell. You guys got everything you need; TV in every cell, air conditioning, baseball every day, shows every week---

Kidney: Screw you. We ain't getting what we want and you know it. Hey, wait, we just got four more hostages.

Warden: Let them go. And I order you back in your cell.

Kidney: Nuts to you.

Warden: I'm calling out the National Guard. Get back. Get back in there.

Kidney: Too late for that.

Warden: I'm calling the Pentagon.

Kidney: Hey, cut the crap, crumb. I want the governor. Get me the governor, and better get a doctor--the bladder is dying.

Warden: What do you mean?

Kidney: We ain't getting what we need, so the bladder is dying. Do I have to spell it out for you, dummy?

Warden: Okay, pick up the phone. The governor is on the line.

Kidney: Hey, you.

Gov: Yes?

Kidney: Hey, we want out of here. Get us out before we blow up the joint.

Gov: Who are you?

Kidney: Never mind who. And stop stalling. You're poisoning us down here with the water. We're tired of waiting for pure water. The bladder is dying right now from all the crap in the water.

Gov: Just a minute. Just a minute. Let's negotiate.

Kidney: Stick it. No negotiate.

Gov: Let's make a deal.

Kidney: No deal. You promised a year ago—

Gov: I'm afraid we can't meet your demands.

Kidney: Then it's curtains for the hostages, everybody. We ain't got long, crumb, and it'll be on your head.

Gov: Well, I'm willing to negotiate. I can let you have some Pepsi, 8–Up, Tag—

Kidney: Come on, cut the crap.

Gov: I can let you have beer, lite, dark, lager—

Kidney: Cut it. Get me the President. I wanna talk to the President.

Gov: I can get you club soda—Evian water—

Kidney: I want the President or we blow the joint up.

Gov: Okay, okay. I have the President on another line. Hold on.

Kidney: Tell him what we want. Get a move on.

Gov: (To President) President, there's a riot down here. What do they want? They want pure water. Yeah, yeah.
         (To Kidney) The President says we have no pure water. Oh wait, wait just a minute. He says he has to ask Nancy.
         (To President) Oh, okay. Okay.

(To Kidney)   Nancy says you can have chicken soup.

Kidney: Chicken soup.   Christ.   Chicken soup. What's it made of?

Gov: Nancy says it's made of chicken.

Kidney: No, dummy, what kind of water.   Jerk.

Gov: (To President)   What kind of water is the soup made with?
(To Kidney)   Nancy says it's made with tap water like all chicken soup.

Kidney: Aw, hell.   Christ sake, can't anybody get this straight.   Tell him we want pure water in the chicken soup, not tap water.

Gov: (To President)   Mr. President, they say they want pure water in the soup.   Yeah.
(To Kidney)   The President says where in hell is he gonna get pure water.   He hasn't even got any for himself.   Oh, wait.   Wait, just a minute.   I think I hear him crying.
(To President)   Oh, Mr. President, did we upset you?   Yes, yes, I know all about your polyps, and Nancy with the--and all--. What?   I should handle it? You want me to handle it?   What does Nancy say? Nancy says NO.   Just say NO?
(To Kidney)   Nancy says, "Just say No."

Kidney: For Christ sake.   That's all he can do, just say No?   That's it!   That's the end--it's curtains.   We can't go on like this any more.   No pure water! That's the last straw!

Vrooom! There is a gigantic explosion as the prison goes up in a great pillar of smoke and fire, as the guard in the watchtower falls from

64

his perch down onto the dry parched earth below
and disappears in a cloud of dust.

THE END!!!

CHAPTER EIGHTEEN

AGING

Doctor to patient: I tell you, you're going to live to be 80.

Patient: But, doctor, I am 80.

Doctor: See, what did I tell you?

We're all interested in staying well and holding back the aging process. We all want to feel good in to our 70's, 80's, and even 90's, and stay out of nursing homes.

I was having dinner with a friend the other day who tells me every time I see her that she is 84 years old. One day I said to her, "Shirley, you know, when I look in the mirror I say, 'you know you're pushing 80.'"

So she said when she looks in the mirror she says, "Oh, so you're still alive?"

We must be doing something right. But without healthy cells we cannot have a long, healthy life. Without good cells and a clean body, we have disease. But the fact is that we ignore all this about cells. Who wants to hear about cells. Let it take care of itself like it's been doing up till now.

But if you want to feel good, younger, and full of pep, get interested. You can do a lot to improve the condition of your cells. It's life! It's your life! Listen.

The aging process begins when cell regeneration and rebuilding slows down. This is caused by the accumulation of waste. This interferes with the nourishment of the cells (Carter).

The body becomes flooded, shocked, and poisoned by its own excrement. The body can't throw off waste fast enough.

Stimulating the glands helps to eliminate the waste. We are equipped with mechanisms that clear toxins from the body. When these channels are clogged, this process slows down, and vital force is gone. Then we become sluggish, tired, and that is when disease sets in.

So what we need is to clean out the sluggish glands and organs. This is what is making us tired all the time, too.

And reflexology does just that; it will clean the sluggish glands and organs. You can do this for yourself. By massaging the pressure points in the hands or feet, we can clean out the sluggish glands and organs.

"Aging comes from neglect and failure," says Dr. Cerney. He says you're not using the fountain of youth within you. We have natural powers within us if we only knew what to do. The Chinese had the answers to this: they stimulated the glands, believed in mental control—mind over matter--and got results ("Acupuncture Without Needles").

You can do this, too. You can get back your health and vitality in this simple way. It won't even cost you a cent. All you need is to devote a few minutes' time to this every day. All you have to do is take that first step to do this. Reflexology of the glands and organs are outlined in Chapters 9 and 11.

So, what can we do to hold back the aging process?

1.   We can cleanse the glands.

2.   Stimulate the organs.

3.   Do a colon cleanse.

4.   Do the liver cleanse.

5.   We can cleanse by fasting.

6.   We can increase our intake of water to purify cells.

7.   We can take carrot and vegetable juices.

8.   We can choose our diet more wisely. Art Buchwald says diet is part of the verb "to die."

"What you eat is exceedingly important to your immune system," says Dr. William Adler of the National Institute on Aging, Baltimore. We should recognize the deficiency of zinc in the elderly (Zinc foods: cheese, liver, meat, poultry, and nuts).

Would you like to know about a nourishing food, a dessert, and a beauty treatment all at the same time? Here is my Peanut Butter Supreme:

1/4 cup peanut butter
1/4 cup almond butter
1/4 cup sunflower butter
2 or 3 tablespoonsful barley syrup or honey

Stir these together while at room temperature and spread on rice cakes. You can say goodbye to cookies after this.

Also, let's get acquainted with the miracle foods; garlic, onions, chlorophyll, bee pollen.

George Burns says you can't help getting older but you don't have to get old.

Not to be downplayed is the role of sex to give us energy, vitality, and long life. Dr. Cerney says that the Chinese have long hidden secrets for keeping the body tuned, sustaining energy, and increasing life span.

The Chinese acupuncturists say by using amazing oriental secret procedures, pressing the right acupuncture points, that sexual pleasure can be enhanced and even made to come alive once more.

By pressing and stimulating points and organs far removed from the genital area, sex vitality can be restored (the spleen, stomach, kidney, liver, solar plexus, lower lumbar, medulla oblongata, as well as the genital area). We all know that when we don't feel well we lose interest in sex.

On impotence it was reported that out of 145 men treated by one researcher, 134 were restored to their former manliness ("Acupuncture Without Needles").

Long hidden secrets of the orient are also available for use in frigidity. Dr. Cerney brought back from China eight techniques (booster shots) that can give you added years of sex life, make you feel and look better, younger, and increase your life span. The stimulation areas are also far removed from the genital area (such as the neck, wrist, tip of tailbone, thyroid, and side of the knee and medulla oblongata).

So anyone desirous of keeping the body tuned, sustaining energy and virility, and prolonging the life span in good health has the option of seeking help from a good acupuncturist.

Certainly the payoff would be tremendous for feeling good and gettng the most enjoyment out of life, and—that's what it's all about!

Dr. Norman Vincent Peale, 89 years old says, "If you keep mentally alive and like to work and don't eat too much and go to bed early and get up early and don't hate anybody, you will live a long time."

CELLS

Hello, hello, Cell? This is Estelle. Estelle.
I'm your neighbor downstairs.

Cell: Never heard of you.

Estelle: Whatje think, you were in this alone?

Cell: Never thought about it.

Estelle: Listen, Cell. It's about time we had
           a talk. I got a call that you're not
           doing too well, and I want to see if I
           can help you.

Cell: Get lost, will ya. I'm too tired to
           care.

Estelle: Now, Cell, wait a minute. I can help
           you. I have just what you need.

Cell: Don't bother me. I'm too tired to
           split one more cell.

Estelle: Wait, wait. Listen, Cell, don't give
           up. I know I can help you. I've
           helped others and they're okay now.

Cell: Whatje say your name was?

Estelle: Estelle.

Cell: I think I heard of you.

Estelle: You must've. I'm the one who goes
           around talking about DNA and RNA and
           all that stuff.

Cell: What on earth is that?

Estelle: That's the stuff that keeps us cells
           going. Baby, if you haven't got that,

71

you ain't got nothing. Which is about where you are now.

Cell: So. What's with the ABC, whatever you said.

Estelle: Without that, you and I can't make it, y'understand?

Cell: Okay, what is it. How do you spell it.

Estelle: Let's see R-I-B. Whatdya have to know for, you gonna write a letter? Anyway, you mean to say you never heard of it? Boy, where you been the last 75 years?

Cell: Okay. What does it do? And make it snappy.

Estelle: What does it do? It's the life blood, that's what. Without that we're nothing.

Cell: Aw right, where do you get that stuff?

Estelle: You get it in your food. Mostly in sardines.

Cell: In sardines?

Estelle: Yeah, sardines.

Cell: What kind?

Estelle: Any kind.

Cell: Do they come in oil?

Estelle: Yeah.

Cell: Do they come in tomato sauce?

Estelle: Yeah.

Cell: Mustard sauce? Sardine oil? Water?

Estelle: Yeah, sure.

Cell: I hate sardines.

Estelle: That's what they all say. Boy, you're
           all alike. Me, I never met a sardine
           I didn't like. And you know what
           else?

Cell: What?

Estelle: Salmon. Salmon has nucleic acid, too.

Cell: Oho, who do you think I am,
           Rockefeller? Hey, get lost and don't
           bother me, will you.

Estelle: Wait, wait. Garlic has it, too.
           Garlic is great for nucleic acid.

Cell: I'm thinking chocolate mousse and
           you're hocking me with garlic.

Estelle: Oh boy, I can't do anything with you.
           Looks like you just want to crawl back
           into bed and stay there.

Cell: You got it, pal. I ain't even got the
           energy to move one single cell out.
           They're laying there piling up almost
           five years now. Let it pile up. I'm
           too tired to care. Oh good, look
           what's coming down. I'm getting a
           fix. Another one of those tranquili-
           zers. Great. Just what I need to put
           me out of my misery. Now scram!

Estelle: Wait, wait, just one more sec. Hey, I
           know this girl who takes celery juice.
           You should see her cells.

Cell: Get lost, already.

Estelle: And you know the greatest picker-
           upper: chlorophyll. I hear that's
           dynamite.

Cell: What the heck is that. Boy, you sure
           come up with the craziest stuff. Now
           leave me be.

Estelle: Hey, hang in there. I'll go call
           upstairs right now and try to get the
           boss to give you some of that. I'm
           sure you'd feel great. I'll get back
           to you. Good luck, kid.

Cell: Hey, don't call me--I'll call you.
           Gee, well, maybe it would be nice to
           have some of that good stuff,
           chlorophyll, shmorophyll. I wish, I
           wish, I wish!

CHAPTER TWENTY

STRESS

"Hastiness and superficiality are the psychic
diseases of the 20th century."
                    Alex I. Solzhenitsyn

All this cleansing is fine. You will be
renewed and feel and look better than you had
ever hoped, and compliments will be flying. But
the battle is not entirely won yet. There's
still the matter of stress.

We have all heard many times over the
expression, 'mind over matter,' and now healers
and health practitioners are telling us that what
we think affects us physically.

Dr. Dennis T. Jaffee of the Saybrook
Institute in San Francisco, says that, "Every
time something upsets you or you feel aggravated,
your body tenses up, muscles tense up, breathing
is shallower, and the whole body gets thrown into
over-drive" ("Future Youth"). That's stress
response.

The first thing to be disrupted when under
stress is the ability to digest food and
consequently extract nutrients in the food. This
brings on destructive, degenerating diseases
because we are not absorbing the nutrients in our
food ("Pursuit of Life").

Worry affects the circulation, heart,
glands, and the whole nervous system.

Dr. John Schindler ("How to Live 365 Days")
says that, "The stress of life today guarantees
that muscular tension in the body will not ease
up—due to circumstances, cares, difficulties,
troubles." He says to stop looking for trouble.
Learn to like work. Have a hobby; learn to like

people. Be satisfied in your situation if you can't easily change it. Learn to accept adversity. Learn to say humorous, cheerful things. Meet your problems with decision.

Dr. Hans Selye says that, "Aging is, in a sense, due to the constant and eventually exhausting stresses of life. Disruption of physiological processes caused by stress may be the villain in many degenerating diseases." Dr. Selye claims that stress can increase triglycerides.

About fatigue—stress causes depletion of iron, resulting in fatigue ("Pursuit of Youth").

Stress releases adrenalin into the bloodstream (and other chemicals) which must be eliminated by action. This theory is known as fight or flight. We must do something about it, even exercise, or taking a walk is good, or else it has side effects like back pain, sprains, or spasms ("Future Youth").

So you don't have to reach for a tranquilizer. Drs. Randolph & Moss say that drugs are a two-million dollar business. They don't cure a problem, but sometimes can cause an illness.

So, what can we do? We can try to slow down. Relax. Relax. Think pleasant thoughts. Picture a peaceful scene.

Since tension seems to be held in the neck and shoulders, do neck stretching exercises. Sit in a chair facing forward and stretch the head up.

Deep heat is good; when muscles tense, the blood is cut off. Take a hot shower. Exercise discharges stress. Imagery, meditation are good for relaxation.

There are calming foods to be taken for stress: sunflower seeds, organ meats, seafood, yeast, eggs, sweet potatoes, whole grains, almonds, sesame seeds, nuts, brown rice, carrots, beets, celery, snap beans, brussel sprouts, chives, alfalfa ("Pursuit of Youth").

Reflexology is very helpful in relieving stress. There are also pressure points on the hands and feet. On the hands, press fingertips of both hands together; hold ten to fifteen minutes.

On feet, press top of feet between second and third toes. (Fig.#4).

Census taker to harried housewife: Madam, I want to know the number of dependents you have, not how many will be alive when their father gets home.

And were you ever told by a doctor to slow down instead of by a policeman?

So relax. Relax. And dare to be different. Dare to do something wonderful for yourself. Don't be like the guy who's afraid to remove the contents tag off his thirty year old mattress!

And ease up. You'll never get out of this world alive!

CHAPTER TWENTY—ONE

ENERGY

"Chronic fatigue is the scourge of modern age."
- Carter

I had a surprise one day by my daughter-in-law. She is in her late 40's, weighs 110 lbs., is a small eater, and consumes a lot of salads. She has worked out in the gym two or three times a week for years.

As a child growing up, she was given vegetable juices to drink every day and lots of raw vegetables to snack on. So she should be in the greatest shape, right? Wrong.

I asked her the other morning if she is ever tired when she wakes up in the morning, and this floored me. She said, "I'm always tired."

The doctors say that this is the biggest complaint they get from their patients, but what can they do? One time, when I was sick with leukemia, I told the doctor I was tired, and he prescribed elavil for me.

I thought this was ridiculous at the time and still think so. He gave me no vitamins, no minerals, no tonics, no blood builders, just an artificial mood elevator. Unbelievable!

I didn't know anything then about pressure points and what wonderful things you can accomplish with massaging the pressure points. I didn't know about releasing toxins from sluggish glands and organs using this method; I didn't know that the liver needed cleansing desperately and the colon was also in need of cleansing!

I didn't know about kelp, a natural nutrient for the thyroid (Dr. Jensen says if you

wake up tired in the morning, you need kelp-
iodine).

And how can you have energy when you have
tired blood? What is tired blood? When toxins
aren't eliminated, they collect in the blood and
the blood becomes progressively more stagnant.

So, what can you do for tired blood? For
energy, massage the endocrine glands (Figure #2),
and then stimulate the organs by applying
pressure to the pressure points in the hands.

Massage the liver and spleen for a half
minute (Figures #3 and #4). Then massage the
pituitary gland in the pad of the thumb.

Berkson & Tuchak ("Zone Therapy") say
simply pulling on the fingers pulls out toxins.
I find this very effective. The finger pull will
give you instant energy.

A sure-fire way to regain energy is to
press a little hand comb into the palm of the
hand and move it around to reach different areas.

A hot/cold shower will give you energy.
Three minutes hot, and 15 to 30 seconds cold.
Repeat 3 to 5 times (ask doctor).

Another helpful hint: Dr. Roger Minkow
("Future Youth") says that creative energy
unleashes energy, even going for a walk. Do
something you like to do.

Napping, too, is good for you. Winston
Churchill napped every afternoon. He said he
could do one and a half day's work in one day.
The best time is from 2 to 3 P.M. It's part of
an internal biorhythm (Berkeley Wellness Letter
10/85).

Mrs. Carter says a quick energy pickup is a wash cloth dipped in cool water and vinegar. After a few minutes, give yourself a quick massage for a new surge of energy.

And now the energy foods: wheat germ, whole grain bread, nuts, potassium, potatoes, bananas, oranges, raisins, flounder, milk, and lean meat.

And Dr. Walker says that apple cider vinegar combines with alkaline elements and minerals to produce energy.

Another treat for the body and for the entire system is carrot juice. Think of it. With a little bit of effort, and for only a few pennies a day, you can do something wonderful for yourself. So, if you want to feel great instead of just sitting there and aging, this is a great thing you can do for your body. See Chapter 32 on carrot juice. This will help you have a renewed body, feel good and young again.

And then there are the miracle foods for good blood and veins; chlorophyll (see chapter on chlorophyll), garlic, bee pollen, honey, gensing, and the new substance germanium (also in another chapter) that has an energizing effect even in small dosages.

So, go to it. It's all right there for you!

CHAPTER TWENTY-TWO

LORD, I'M BACK

Me: Hello, Lord. I'm back.

Lord: Well, well, come in. How did you make out.
Tell me, I'm anxious to hear. Are they
listening to you? Is anyone following your
advice, your footsteps? Is anyone getting
any better? Tell me, I can't wait to hear.

Me: Lord, I'm a miserable flop.

Lord: Why? What's happening?

Me: Lord, they laughed at me. I'm so
embarrassed.

Lord: So—that's how it is. They won't listen to
you. They just laugh. Hmm! Can you beat
that! Everyone wants to get well, feel
younger, beat aging, but they don't want to
bother to do anything about it. Remarkable!
I can't believe it.

Me: Believe, believe. I tried. I really
tried. Advertised this stuff all over the
place. They listen, then they turn away.
Do you know what they say? They say they
never had to do these things up till now,
so they're not going to start now.

Lord: Are you sure you told them how good it
would make them feel? Boy, that sure is a
stubborn bunch down there; tell me again,
what did you tell them?

Me: Lord, I told them sure they never did this
before, but that they were never 75 years
old before. Now is when you need this, I
said. You need all the help you can get, I
told them. But, nothing. No response.

Lord: This really bothers me. Here, all these people are retired--the oldies, I mean. They're retired and they won't spend a half hour a day on their health! And you are right. They're the ones who need it most.

Me: Lord, of course; of course they have plenty of time. They have loads of time. They even complain that they're bored, have nothing to do. And look, don't they wait for hours in the doctor's office--an hour or two every time they go?

Lord: Well, I guess it's where your priorities are. I don't know where this is going to end.

Me: Lord, I've got to tell you this. One man was stooped over and in pain--couldn't straighten up. So I told him about the cleanses. Several times I told him this might help him. And do you know what he said? He said, "When I'll die, I'll die!" Case closed.

Lord: Hmm. Hmm. Let me see. Did you tell everybody I'll give them a few extra years? They should go for that.

Me: That's the first thing I said. But, look nobody wants to do it. Nobody. They just say they never did it before, and they don't want to start now to make new habits.

Lord: It depresses me, I tell you. Do you think I enjoy seeing these miserable wrecks complaining this hurts, that hurts, every day something else? And running to doctors every day. You think I like that? You call that living, the way they drag themselves around, and always tired! I can't stand it, I tell you. Wait. Wait.

I have another idea. Suppose I sweeten the
pot again? Suppose I throw in another
bonus?

Me: It'll have to be good.

Lord: Yes, yes, maybe this will do it. Suppose
you go back and tell them that if they'll
do this program, I will take away their
wrinkles. So they'll feel better and also
look young again. How's that? I'll turn
back the aging clock for them.

Me: Great, Lord. Great. But—can you do that?

Lord: Can I do it? Why, I'm the Lord, Creator of
the Universe. But a magician I'm not. If
they will do it, I will be glad to help
them. But if they won't cooperate, I
cannot help them.

Me: Lord, I'm impressed. I'm going back down
there and tell them what you said. Maybe
they'll listen now.

Lord: Good. And don't forget to tell them about
all the miracle foods I provided them with.
And let me hear from you soon. Real soon.
Good luck!

Well, it sure looks like some of it is up to us!

CHAPTER TWENTY-THREE

BEAUTY

Several years ago I met a lady whose complexion was peaches and cream. When I asked her what she does to have that beautiful skin, she answered that you have to be born with it.

That may be so, but I find that after being on the colon cleanse program on and off for the past several months, taking coffee enemas, regularly juicing carrots, spinach, and beets, I find that my complexion is improving, and the skin is tightening up.

So—beauty comes from within. I have had facial acupuncture, done facial exercises to get rid of wrinkles and folds, and have taken expensive collagen treatments. But nothing tightens and smooths the skin like the colon cleanse.

Dr. Forsyth (the colon specialist) says the colon cleanse can remove wrinkles and tighten the skin. And who wouldn't want that. Think of that the next time you see those wrinkles in the mirror.

Also, people who don't get enough sleep have dull looking skin because they're not giving their bodies enough time to produce new fresh skin cells. While we sleep, our skin repairs itself, according to Nancy Durr, Research Associate for a New York dermatologist.

Drinking water also helps maintain proper muscle tone. It plumps the skin, leaving it clear, healthy, resilient.

Applying honey to the face and leaving it on for 20 minutes is a natural skin balm. You can do this even 20 times a day.

84

Also, with reflexology, you can give yourself a beauty treatment by applying acupressure to get the blood moving to the head. This is also good for the face, eyes, ears, and memory--and all of us seniors need help in these areas.

To do this, we start by massaging the neck. There is an artery going down from the ear--the carotid artery. Massage lightly in a downward stroke and tilt your head in the opposite direction at the same time (Figure #5).

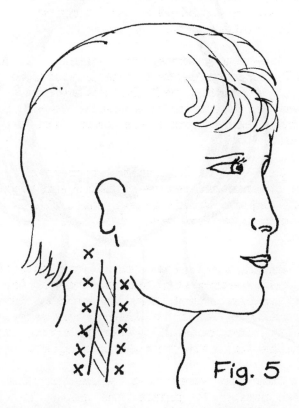

Fig. 5

Then go to the sides of the carotid artery and apply pressure at the site of the X's (Figure #5).

85

Then go to the front of the neck, alongside the Adams apple and at the bottom of the neck (Figure #6).

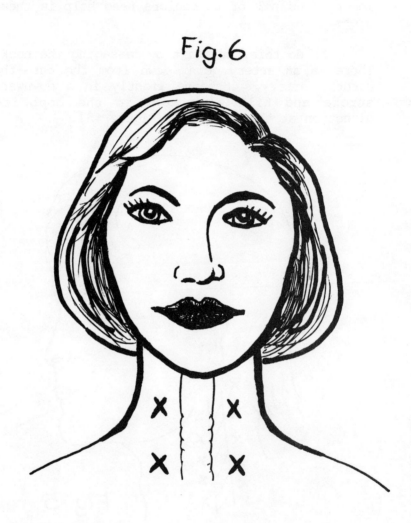

Fig. 6

Then go to the back of the neck and apply pressure in the center groove just where the neck meets the head. Hold for a few seconds, release, then press again (Figure #7).

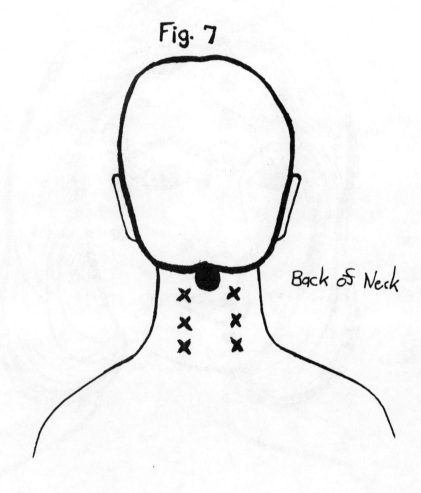

Fig. 7

Back of Neck

All this will get the blood flowing to the head.

Now we go to the pressure points in the
face as shown in Figure #8. Hold each point for
a count of three. Do this three times.

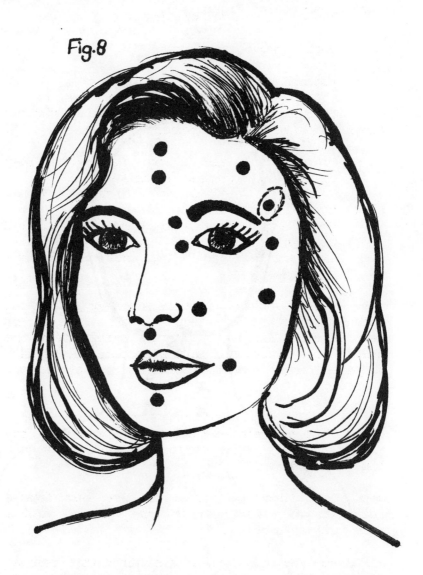

Fig.8

Then with gentle pressure, make a circle at
the temples, alongside of the end of the
eyebrows. Apply gentle pressure while making
circles.

When finished, pat the whole face with a quick tapping motion of the fingertips and then smooth it all down with the fingertips.

Beauty comes from within.

Health comes from within.

Youthfulness comes from within.

Certain foods also are especially rich in minerals to enhance and beautify the skin:

Rice polish has 90 mg. niacin for rosy cheeks, 10 mg. thiamin for texture.
Oat bran has 30 mg. thiamin, 20 mg. magnesium for cells.
Yellow corn meal with lysine has 15 mg. thiamin.
Rice flour has 15 mg. niacin, 10 mg. thiamin.

Barley water is an aid for beautiful skin. Queen Elizabeth drinks barley water every day of her life. But I get barley syrup (from the health food store) and take a spoonful every day, and what can be more pleasant than licking it off a spoon.

Phyllis Diller says she was ugly as a child, but her mother told her beauty is on the inside. So she asked her mother, "So why wasn't I born inside out?"

One night she prayed to have skin like a teenager. The next morning she woke up with a face full of pimples.

So--you only need a dedication to a renewal of yourself.

Do it--it's easy!

CHAPTER TWENTY-FOUR

ST. PETER TALKS WITH SATAN

St. Peter: Hello, hello, is this Satan?

Satan: Ah, yes. With whom do I have the pleasure?

St. Peter: Come off it, Sate. You know darn well, and the fact is I think it's high time we had another little chat before the whole world passes into extinction.

Satan: Oh, hey, I love that. Say it again. "Passes into extinction." Wow!

St. Peter: Cut it out, Sate. Let's be serious.

Satan: I was never more serious in my life-- er, life. Listen, this is fun time for me.

St. Peter: Satan, now look here, you've had your fun. Many times over.

Satan: I know, I know. Let's see; the last time I ever had fun was the flu epidemic. But that was so long ago. Hey, maybe we can stir up another one like that. I have to think about that.

St. Peter: You're impossible.

Satan: Are you kidding? Listen, I can't help it if people are stupid and greedy. Why, they just fall at my feet by the thousands, maybe millions. Ah, I love it!

St. Peter: You're sick. You've been raising too
much er-hell around here; you gotta
stop.

Satan: Pete, that's what keeps my blood
flowing in my head.

St. Peter: Sate, you're the most selfish devil I
ever met.

Satan: Pete, you can't stop me now. I'm on a
roll. Boy, I've waited a long time
for this.

St. Peter: Hey, Sate, give us a break, will you?

Satan: What do you mean, Pete?

St. Peter: You gotta do me a big favor. You
gotta do this for me.

Satan: Pete, you're dreaming. I ain't
promising nothing.

St. Peter: You gotta do this one time for me.
Believe me you won't be sorry.

Satan: What are you talking about?

St. Peter: I'm talking about saving the people.
Look, after they're all gone, you'll
have nothing to work with. Look at it
that way. Doesn't that make sense?

Satan: I ain't listening.

St. Peter: Sate, listen, you got to talk to the
big boys for me. You know, the big
corporations.

Satan: Yeah? What about? I talk to them
every day. Who do you think is behind

them telling them what to do, their wives? Ha! Stop kidding me, Pete.

St. Peter: Sate, put down that pitchfork a minute and listen. Your big boys are poisoning the people with all the pesticides and sprays in the food.

Satan: Yeah, ah, yes. That's music to my ears.

St. Peter: And that's not all. They're poisoning the water, too.

Satan: Tell me more. I love it.

St. Peter: And they're planning on using radio-active isotopes in a lot of our food very soon.

Satan: Yeah, those are my boys you're talking about. They can do no wrong. Get lost, Pete.

St. Peter: Okay, Sate, if you're not gonna listen to reason, I'll just have to give the people something to protect them-selves. That's the only way I can see out of it.

Satan: Hey, hold it right there, Peter. This time I fixed it so you can't do anything to spoil my act.

St. Peter: Oh, really! Well, I still have a few tricks of my own. I'm not just gonna sit around here whistling Dixie and watch you blow them all away.

Satan: What you got in mind, Pete? Not that it will work, mind you. You don't scare me none.

St. Peter: Thought you'd never ask, Sate. Well, here goes. You've had your fun, and now I have to warn the people. Hell—I mean Heaven—I don't need any more up here, and you certainly have enough down there.

Satan: What are you thinking?

St. Peter: If you don't turn your big boys off, I'm gonna have to use my big guns.

Satan: Like what?

St. Peter: Are you ready for this?

CHAPTER TWENTY-FIVE

ANSWER TO SATAN

Satan: Well, Pete, let me hear about your, hahaha-er, big guns.

St. Peter: Sate, we got an awful lot of things to defend ourselves with. And let me mention yogurt first.

Satan: Hohoho, and I thought you were serious. Hahaha!

St. Peter: Hold it, Sate. Looks like you don't know what it's for. Listen:

Yogurt neutralizes most poisons. Specifically, it neutralizes DDT. Also, Strontin 90 And toxic drugs.

Satan: You don't say.

St. Peter: And we have kelp.

Satan: Oh boy, you need help, not kelp.

St. Peter: Looks like you don't know anything about kelp either. Kelp is an excellent protector against Strontin 90.

Satan: Well, how about that!

St. Peter: Then we have lecithin. This neutralizes all body poisons. It also helps counteract the effect of X-rays. Get that?

Then we have Vitamin B complex. This protects against many toxic residues in food.

What do you say? How do you like it
so far?

Satan: I'm not listening.

St. Peter: Then we have B15. This protects
against air pollution, smog, especially carbon monoxide. Sate, we know
you're doing your darndest to poison
us with polluted air.

Satan: You're talking to a wall.

St. Peter: Then we have Pantothenic acid. This
protects against radiation injuries.

Vitamin C is our best general anti-
toxin. It protects all glands and
organs.

Satan: You're still harping on that C stuff.
Boy, am I tired of hearing about that.

St. Peter: Then we have Vitamin E. It's a
protector against polluted air.

It helps the liver in its detoxifying
work. It protects against most
poisons in food, water, and air.

Get that, Sate? It's Vitamin E I'm
talking about.

Satan: So—

St. Peter: Then we have Vitamin A. This protects
against smog—pollution.

Vitamin A works with calcium, one of
the most important antitoxins.

And, Sate, don't forget the biggie—
garlic!

95

Satan: Yeah. Wake me up when you're through.

St. Peter: And now for some real strong stuff. It's a wonderfully powerful herb to counteract all that radiation. I'm sure you've never heard of it. It's violet leaf tea.

Satan: I can handle that.

St. Peter: And here's our best! Here's the most amazing miracle stuff the whole world has been waiting for.

Satan: You know you're boring me.

St. Peter: Oh, Sate, just wait till you get a load of this.

Satan: Really! You don't say!

St. Peter: What we have for you now, Sate, is a most miraculous miracle. Not much is known about it yet, but what is known is that it's the last word in miracle healers. It's **GERMANIUM!**

Satan: GERMANIUM! OOOOW! DRAT! Foiled again!

Hehehe.

FADE OUT!

CHAPTER TWENTY-SIX

GERMANIUM

We seniors need all the help we can get,
and there's good news in sight!

There's a new kid on the block, but it's
not just an ordinary kid. It's not a vitamin,
not a mineral, not a drug. It's a substance.
Studies show it can cure, heal, stimulate,
invigorate, rejuvenate, and has the same miracle
powers as the waters of the Shrine at Lourdes in
France, where many people have been known to
visit for cures.

The new substance is called Germanium. The
late Dr. Asai discovered it and first tested it
on himself. It cured his chronic arthritis in
weeks.

Tests done on Germanium have shown that the
good news about it is endless. It has shown to
have near-miraculous effects on human health--
and is related to the production of interferon.

Tests show:

It is a versatile sustainer of human
health.

It is a dramatic enhancer of immunity.

It is an effective anti-cancer agent.

It helps expel pollutants from the body.

It has amazing curative powers.

It could apparently invigorate, rejuvenate, restore sexual function, heal burns
without scarring, cure radiation sickness, restore eyesight and hearing, heal

97

cancers, circulatory disorders including heart attacks, stroke—all responded well to Germanium.

Further, it normalizes blood pressure, immune function, has an effect on cholesterol, triglycerides, and brings hemoglobin up and white count down.

It is shown to have antiviral and anti-tumor effects.

It is a potent anti-cancer agent.

It consistently has an energizing effect even in small doses.

It is called the ultimate nutrient.

It is non-toxic, highly safe, and completely harmless.

Germanium is now being tested for many other diseases. Already in North America there exists anecdotal reports of its amazing effects on human health—well named, a miracle cure.

Dr. Asai said Germanium restores health to those afflicted with disease and sustains health in those who are healthy.

The National Cancer Institute has announced its acceptance of Germanium as a new approach in the treatment of cancer and AIDS for research purposes and many health authorities are already saying that Germanium can possibly cure almost every conceivable disease know to man.

There is still much research being done on Germanium.

Some kid!

CHAPTER TWENTY-SEVEN

LEG PAINS

Leg pains are quite common in the elderly. "When you eat three fatty meals a day, there's continuous sludging, resulting in poor oxygen and other nutrients. Symptoms are leg pains, fatigue, difficulty in walking, etc." (The McDougall Plan). For leg pains, Jason Winters recommends coffee enemas.

The Council on Nutritional Research says that the kidney must strain impure water. Kidneys must work day and night. If the kidneys fail to strain these poisons out, you see the effects all through your body, thickened joints, painful nerves, weakened arteries, rheumatism, various disturbances of circulation.

So leg pains could conceivably come from drinking impure water. Citrus fruit is recommended for its bio-flavinoids.

And now for some help from reflexology:

Mrs. Carter recommends massaging the colon areas on the feet. (See Figure #9.)

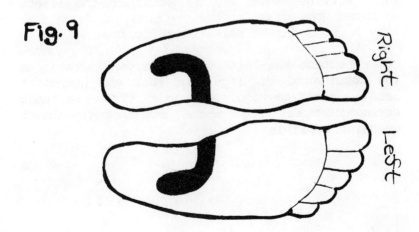

Fig. 9   Right   Left

Also for instant relief from cramping, press cords directly in back of the knee.

For leg pain, also massage under back part of foot. (See Figure #10.)

Fig. 10

Various veins are connected to the liver, so treat the liver. Use caution at first, as many poisons can be released at first.

Massage the legs by applying pressure along the outside of the legs, the back and inside of legs. And, of course, don't sit with legs crossed; raise legs above level of the heart whenever possible.

CHAPTER TWENTY-EIGHT

EYES

I was having lunch with a friend one day, and she mentioned that someone we both knew was having a cataract operation. And then we remarked that so many people were having cataract operations. Dr. Julian Shulman ("Cataracts") says that half a million cataract operations are performed yearly. It is considered a normal part of aging.

During the conversation we recalled that our parents who lived well into their 80's didn't have cataract operations and neither did anyone else we knew who were in their age group. True, they wore eyeglasses, but that was all the eye correction we had ever heard of at that time.

So how come people rarely needed a cataract operation then, and now these operations are so prevalent? On questioning, we found that there are many more causes of eye deterioration now than there were years ago.

Some sources: radiation! We're getting radiation in the home from microwave ovens, colored TV sets, from wall smoke alarms, and from fluorescent lighting.

Drs. Ecker and Bramesco ("Radiation") say that microwave or radar radiation in sufficient doses over sufficient periods of time can result in the formation of cataracts. They say also that a combination of heat and nonthermal mechanisms is probably responsible for cataracts and damage to the lenses of the eyes--such as the retina.

There are many other indoor irritants which, even at extremely low levels, irritate the eyes, nose, and throat (formaldehyde, insulation, perma press clothes, toothpaste, air fresheners, cosmetics). One fifth of the population is affected to some degree.

Sprays from air freshener cans can damage the cornea of the eyes from the chemical particles. Car exhausts, airport pollution can result in blurring of vision ("Alternate Approach to Allergies," Drs. Randolph & Moss).

Sunlight also may cause cataracts and other eye diseases. Eyeglasses offer some protection.

So much for outside sources that damage the eye. But our own physiology has its effect on the eyes; poisons in our bodies contribute, says Jason Winters. Degenerative changes in the eyes, cataracts, and bloodshot eyes, he says, come from poisons in the intestines and colon. Aha!

Mr. Winters says there are 36 poisons in the alimentary canal and they can cause degenerative changes in the eyes, inflammation of the lens and hardening of the lens, cataracts, eyes dull and heavy, and other symptoms.

Dr. Forsyth ("The Perfect Cleanse") says she has seen eye problems greatly improved when the bowels were cleansed.

Also, some medications cause cataracts, like the long term use of cortisone ("Cataracts").

And, since the eyes are under the control of the nervous system, when the nerves are fatigued, the eyes function imperfectly.

Is there any help? Yes, there is, but you must be under the supervision of your eye doctor. At the same time, you can learn of the foods that are good for eyes.

Do you know what these foods have in common? Sweet potatoes, cantaloupes, carrots, apricots? They all have carotene. Also good for the eyes are parsley, spinach, broccoli, beef liver, meat, chicken, sunflower seeds, brown rice, and whole grains.

Dr. Walker says that parsley juice is efficient in every ailment connected with the eyes and optic nerve system. Weak eyes, ulceration of the cornea, cataracts have been effectively treated by drinking raw parsley juice.

But parsley juice must never be taken alone. It must be mixed with other juices. Taken with other juices it is extremely beneficial.

And now a little help from reflexology.

For eye strain, rotate the big toe round and round till relieved.

Dr. Cerney says to grab all the toes in one hand and manipulate them up and down, then slap the bottoms of the feet.

Dr. Julius Shulman ("Cataracts") says that cataracts can come from the improper working of the glands in the neck.

With a gentle downward motion, stroke carotid artery on sides of the neck (Figure #5).

On hands, apply pressure to points as shown in Figure #3. Press and deeply massage web between 2nd and 3rd fingers. Press and hold this site for several minutes twice a day. (A simple way to do this is to apply a clothespin to the web and leave it on for a few minutes.)

For instant relief, hold tips of 2nd and 3rd fingers several minutes. You can do this with clothespins and also with rubber bands applied to the tips of these fingers.

On the face, press and make small circles on the inner corner of the eye. Massage and rotate little circles on the bony areas around the eyes, on eyebrows and under the eyes.

Look at all the wonderful things you can do for the eyes!

CHAPTER TWENTY-NINE

EARS

The other day, while browsing in the library, I came across a beautiful impressive-looking 24-page booklet on loss of hearing, published by a senior citizen group boasting members in the millions. I took the booklet home, scanned every page hoping for any hint of a natural aid to better hearing that you could do for yourself, but there was none.

It explained what happens to our hearing as we age, the different age groups when ear deterioration is most common, and advised that you see your physician, and if necessary, an ear doctor.

The little booklet said not one word about self-healing, and I wondered if it was possible to do something for yourself naturally that would help loss of hearing, and after pursuing this, I found the following:

Dr. Cerney ("Acupuncture Without Needles") says that the Chinese and the French have had remarkable success with hearing problems using acupuncture. So it is possible to get relief naturally with acupuncture.

Mrs. Carter ("Hand Reflexology") says she has seen deafness cured by just tying a rubber band around the ring finger. It must be tied around the tip of the finger. Leave on for a few minutes and remove before the finger turns blue. Do this on both hands and as many times a day as you wish.

Interestingly, in China, a health team in 1968 sought a cure for deafness using acupuncture. They found that repeated insertion of needles just behind the ear restored the function of damaged nerves. Deaf mutes began to hear

105

almost immediately, many for the first time in their lives ("Acupuncture," Marc Duke).

Dr. Cerney ("Acupuncture Without Needles") says that aging comes from neglect and failure-- you're not using the fountains of youth within you.—It's the failure to use the natural powers within yourself. So, stimulate the glands, think positive, and perhaps a little acupuncture might help.

With regard to diet: eat less fat, less salt. Eat fish, fiber, Vitamin D, and of course, no smoking.

And, about the new kid on the block-- Germanium, the new miracle substance. It is shown to have a great benefit on the ears. See chapter on Germanium.

I love holistic!

CHAPTER THIRTY

CHOLESTEROL

Following are reports from the University of California, Berkeley Wellness Letters regarding cholesterol:

Vegetable oils and peanut butter have no cholesterol since they're not animal products (1/87).

Certain oils lower cholesterol--olive, corn, safflower, soybean, sunflower (9/86).

Garlic oil inhibits coagulation of blood, and garlic may actually be used as a weapon on heart disease. Garlic reduces level of cholesterol (10/85).

Beans, legumes, oat bran; these seem to inhibit the absorption of cholesterol into the bloodstream (9/86).

Fiber in raw fruits, raw vegetables, nuts, brown rice, avocado, barley, oats, lower cholesterol. Drink liquid with these (8/85).

Eggplant binds with cholesterol for removal from the body. Oats and beans, if eaten regularly, can dramatically lower serum cholesterol. One quarter pound of beans daily or one serving oatmeal plus 5 oatmeal muffins daily. But oatmeal for breakfast and bean soup for lunch is acceptable, three times weekly (1/86).

The best low fat, low cholesterol desserts: frozen yogurt, ice milk, sherbet, ices, contain no fat, no cholesterol (7/85).

You can make butter equal to margarine. Each tablespoon will have 5 grams polyunsaturated fat, approximately the same as in most better margarines. Simply mix equal amounts of softened butter and polyunsaturated oil and chill (10/85).

And K.K. Sharma, an Indian Scientist, says onions and garlic carry off harmful cholesterol. You don't have to eat them raw.

Also, Jason Winters recommends yucca tablets for lowering cholesterol and trigly-cerides.

CHAPTER THIRTY-ONE

CHLOROPHYLL

There's so much we don't know about the miracle foods that were put here for us on this planet, and chlorophyll is one of them.

It is made from alfalfa. You can get alfalfa tablets or alfalfa sprouts, but I like the liquid alfalfa, chlorophyll. You can take more of it that way, and besides, you can always have it on hand.

Want to know what it does for you? It is great for the entire body:

It stimulates bone marrow.

It has a direct action on the cells.

It enables the body to digest and utilize food, thus increasing resistance to sickness and old age.

It improves appetite and digestion.

Bowel movements become regular.

Condition of the heart improves.

It stimulates tissue growth.

It prevents hardening of the arteries.

It has spectacular results in sinus and chronic conditions.

The heart beat improves with chlorophyll and it aids flexibility.

Dr. K. Birsher, Research Scientist, says, "Chlorophyll increases the function of the heart, affects the vascular system, the intestines, the uterus, and lungs--and considering its stimulating properties, cannot be compared with any other." This is backed up with carefully documented studies.

Distinguished scientists agree that they have seen chlorophyll combat deep-lying infection with no irritating effects.

Investigators at Temple University in Philadelphia said, "The green solution seemed to thicken and strengthen the walls of the cells of living animals."

As a result of this interesting research, many distinguished physicians and surgeons now prescribe chlorophyll. The most spectacular results occur in the treatment of chronic sinus infections and head colds. In 1,000 cases treated under the supervision of Drs. Ridpath and Davis, prominent specialists, they reported, "There is not a single case in which either improvement or cure has not taken place."

Before 1950, liquid chlorophyll was unknown as a tonic until Paul DeSouza introduced it to the U.S. health food stores. He is a pioneer health food enthusiast and exponent of natural, organic farming methods which are in wide usage today as a result of his energy and determination. He grows alfalfa on his farm, bottles it, and owns and operates a natural and pure food produce manufacturing warehouse in California.

In 1979 he was awarded the Certificate of Merit for distinguished achievement and received a commendation.

All of the above is quoted from Chlorophyll Research Bulletin by Nutrition Research.

Chlorophyll!   A miracle food we know
nothing about. We have been missing out on some
of the best aids to good health. And now we can
help ourselves with this miracle food.

Take chlorophyll with grape or cranberry
juice. As much as four tablespoons to a glass.

And, enjoy good health!

CHAPTER THIRTY-TWO

CARROT JUICE

Dr. N.W. Walker ("Fresh Vegetable and Fruit Juices") says to bear in mind that juices are the very finest nourishment we can get, and if we continue to take them as long as we live, the chances are that we will live a healthier life much longer than we would without them. Carrot juice has the same molecules as blood molecules.

Linus Pauling says, "Molecules are in the brain," a most interesting and revealing fact.

Did you say you're tired all the time? Well, carrot juice is indeed a miracle food for you.

> It has the effect of normalizing the entire system.

> It protects the nervous system.

> It is unequalled for increasing vigor and vitality.

> It helps prevent infections of the eyes and throat as well as the sinuses and the respiratory organs generally.

A lady asked me the other day why couldn't she just eat a carrot; why do you have to juice it. "Eating is good," I told her, "but today, I juiced two pounds of carrots."

The wonderful part of taking juices is that they don't have to be digested. You get the benefits of all the natural vitamins and minerals immediately.

Also, any toxins or pesticides remain in the fiber, which is discarded, so the juice is absolutely pure.

Carrot juice is a quick picker-upper. Since it doesn't have to be digested, it enters the bloodstream immediately, bursting forth with all the freshness and health giving elements to be found.

And Dr. John Kelley says, "By juicing, you have immediate access to vast amounts of vitamins and minerals."

One pint of carrot juice daily has more value than 25 pounds of calcium tablets (Walker).

Raw carrot juice is a natural solvent for ulcerous and cancerous conditions (Walker).

I can hear you saying you don't want to bother with this. You've gotten along all these years without all this stuff; and who wants to think about this anyway.

Well, the truth is, and I'll say it again, you've never been 70-75 years old before; you've never been so clogged up before; you've never needed help to survive in good health before. Think about it if you want to feel better, live longer.

So—you need a juicer! Ask yourself, "Am I worth it?" We go out to expensive restaurants, order expensive dinners, so why not the luxury of a juicer? You say you don't want to bother? Again, say, "Am I worth it?" Are good health, good looks, and beating old age worth it?

And look at the payoff you'll get—wow! You've been doing it your way all these years, so why not give this a try?

There's a little hole-in-the-wall store in my city where an 89 year old man makes vegetable juices. He bottles them in quart size bottles and sends them over to his private customers in Palm Beach (smart people!).

Perhaps you can find someone in your area who does this. Or else it's a good money making opportunity for anyone looking for some extra cash--home delivery. This little old man treated me to a cup of carrot juice, and it was so sweet, it tasted like there was honey in it.

I like to mix carrots with other vege-tables. Spinach is a great cleanser. Celery is a diuretic and improves the health of the cells.

Fresh beets are good for the blood, and I try to have some on hand all the time. However, if you're starting to juice beets, you must use very little at first as beets have a powerful cleansing effect on the liver, and you might experience a little nausea (Walker).

So, carrot juice for healthy cells--for long life!

There's a sign in the little old man's store:

**DON'T WAIT TILL IT'S TOO LATE
TO START JUICE THERAPY!**

CHAPTER THIRTY-THREE

SALT, AH, SALT

You like salt? You miss it in your food? And you'd love to have it in your food once again? Well, what about salt? And why can't we have it? Let's look into it.

The Bible talks about salt:

Lev. 2:13 — Shalt thou season with salt.

Ezr. 6:19 — Wheat, salt, wine and oil.

Job 6:6 — Can that which is unsavory be eaten without salt?

Luke 14:34 — Salt is good.

Col. 4:6 — Seasoned with salt.

Natural salt, the type that is solar evaporated and not oven or kiln-dried, was used during Biblical times long before processing and packaging were ever thought about.

At one time in history, salt was used in bartering, same as money is used today.

Now, let's see what the doctors say:

Dr. Walker says that salt is necessary in the generation and function of the digestive fluids in the system. Without salt, good digestion is virtually impossible, but such salt must be entirely soluble in water. (This seems to be the crux of the matter.)

In the processing of the manufactured salt, several chemicals are added that are not completely soluble in water. Hence, the salt is not soluble in water.

Salt that will not dissolve in water cannot dissolve in the body, and therefore has a tendency to collect in the body organs. Natural salt will not clog your system. Whatever salt your body doesn't need will then be eliminated by your body as easily as you eliminate other substances (Walker).

Dr. Loughran says in "Ninety Days to a Better Heart" that salt may be used in moderation. Salt is the only commonly used substance from which the body can make hydrochloric acid. Most middle agers do not have enough.

When salt is withheld, weakness and sickness follow. Even a salt-restricted diet causes weakness which naturally increases the aging process (Salt report).

So the truth is that we cannot live without salt. The body makes needed hydrochloric acid from salt and this acid is one of the digestive juices that we must have.

Salt, also, has a tendency to dissolve the damaging calcium deposits through the entire body.

Okay. Salt is good. Salt is necessary. Now let's see what kind of salt we've been eating and what it does to the body.

About 50 years ago the major producing companies in the United States began to dry their salt in huge kilns. The temperature reached as high as 1200-1500 degrees Fahrenheit. This changes the chemical structure of the salt and the calcium in the salt is damaged. Then the body tries to use it and fails. The result is calcification or hardening of the arteries.

All of the salt we have, unfortunately, is "kiln dried." This means dried at temperatures as high as 1200 to 1500 degrees. This salt has a tendency to collect in the body organs and trouble starts. This results in malfunctioning of body chemical processes and among these would be heart disease, arthritis, and hardening of the arteries; also calcium deposits in the joints and muscle tissue (inflammation).

So the drying of salt and the chemicals that are added during processing are what prevents the salt from dissolving in water; and what will not dissolve in water will not dissolve in the body.

Today heart disease and arthritis are so prevalent that even small children suffer.

But—you're not going to believe this: in countries such as Mexico, China, India, heart disease and arthritis are so rare that many doctors HAVE NEVER SEEN A CASE! These countries do not alter their salt supply. They do not have the machinery to do so. They eat their salt in its natural state as it comes from the mine or is dried from the ocean by the sun's rays (Quoted from Natural Research, Calimesa, California). Hmmm!!!

Natural salt is unheated and untreated; it has been cured by nature for thousands of years in the earth which is the great purifier. It has a delightful flavor.

So—what to do? It's so simple you only have to know. Use rock salt. Grind or crush it to pulverize it. Also, check with your doctor and...

Enjoy in good health!

CHAPTER THIRTY-FOUR

INSOMNIA

Many older people suffer from insomnia, and this can sap your energy. There are a few things you can do naturally to help bring on sleep.

Why do we need enough sleep? Sleep speeds healing; speeds tissue renewal. Cell division is fastest when we are asleep, and the immune system is helped to be more efficient when we have enough sleep. Sleep also aids the memory.

What can we do to bring on sleep? There are foods that contain tryptophan which produces serotonin which helps you sleep. Some of these foods are:

Nuts, seeds, organ meats, brown rice, cereal, carrots, beets, celery, snap beans, chives, alfalfa, brussel sprouts, and especially sesame seeds. Eat halvah. I find my peanut butter recipe puts me to sleep.

Some important minerals for sleep are:

B Complex, thiamin, riboflavin, and niacin.

Lack of these can produce fatigue and sleeplessness.

Here's what the doctors say:

Dr. Michael Stevenson ("Future Youth"), Director of the Insomnia Clinic in Holy Cross Hospital, says, a banana and milk or a small tuna sandwich both contain carbohydrates that produce tryptophan. Take it before bedtime.

Dr. John Kelley (Council on Nutritional Research) says, "If you awaken at night and can't go back to sleep try eating whole grain cereal before bed instead of at breakfast so you'll have enough slow burning carbohydrates to carry you through the night."

A cup of soup or milk at bedtime draws blood into the digestive organ and away from the brain.

Dr. Jarvis says, "Apple cider vinegar and honey can bring on sleep."

Jason Winters says, "A colon cleanse relieves sleeplessness."

A hot bath before bed also relaxes the body. Rub the body after the bath with a mixture of apple cider vinegar and oil.

A hot foot bath before bedtime relaxes the body while rejuvenating the entire body, especially the digestion, lungs, and skin.

Meditation is excellent for falling asleep. There are many tapes available to help bring on sleep.

More tips:

Read something boring.
Listen to quiet, soft music.
Go to bed when tired, sleepy.
Exercise will help you sleep.
Doing something interesting (a hobby) is helpful for sleep.
Boredom can disrupt sleep.
A support system helps.
Deep breathing helps. Also clears the mind.

Then there is reflexology to help you
sleep.   Dr. Cerney ("Acupuncture Without
Needles") says:

Massage web between thumb and forefinger.
Massage wrist 1/4 inch from pinkie side.
Press outside of eyebrows.
Dig index finger into back of neck where
head meets the spine, one finger breadth
away from spine on each side.

Mrs. Carter says to press fingertips of
both hands together and hold for 15 minutes.

Bergson & Tuchak ("Zone Therapy") say to
interlock fingers and hold no less than 10
minutes.

Also, stroke forearms on all surfaces
with fingernails for five to ten minutes.
Press with thumb and index finger above
bridge of nose. Hold ten minutes.

Here's one of my favorite sleep recipes:

To a bowl of spaghetti add:

1 or 2 cloves chopped garlic
Add oil or tomato sauce, yogurt, olives
and chopped parsley, and sleep like a
baby!

It tastes good, too!

CHAPTER THIRTY-FIVE

DIABETES

Dr. Frank's "No Aging Diet" has helped a variety of diseases that lead to old age; emphysema, heart, diabetes, arthritis, and memory.

His diet consists of three sardine meals, one salmon, one liver, and one other seafood meal each week. He has had much success treating diseases with this diet, with patients from teenagers to people in their 80's.

He says his patients look younger and feel younger.

What Dr. Frank's diet does is supply the body with nucleic acid, RNA, and DNA.

He says that white flour products clog up the system, resulting in diabetes, arthritis, coronary, hemorrhoids, and varicose veins. Antidote: celery juice. Celery juice is the secret to better health!

And, of course, a colon cleanse and fasting once a week can only be of help in speeding up the regenerating process.

Actually, it's as if the whole picture of good health is opening up; there are so many ways to get well and keep well. And ways we never knew about!

A mixture of brussel sprout juice with carrots, string beans, and lettuce regenerates the insulin producing properties of pancreatic function. This is of inestimable benefit for diabetes. But the body must be cleansed first. (Dr. Walker).

Foods to eat:

Calf liver, potatoes with skin, whole grain bread, vegetables, cheese, chicken legs, and up to 2,000 mgs. Vitamin C. Combine this with exercises, starting with moderate exercise, and continue it regularly, if possible.

And consult with your doctor on any new course. So—there is help all around, if only we know what to do!

CHAPTER THIRTY-SIX

FOOD

Why must we accept as normal what we see in a race of sick and weakened individuals?

We have seen that enervation causes poisons to be retained in the blood, and this is the enemy. One way to fight the enemy is with certain foods. (See how many ways there are to get rid of poisons!)

Dr. Abram Hoffer ("Orthomolecular Nutrition") says that as long as food processing continues to strip out essential nutrients, there will be no let up in chronic ill health. Every decade a larger portion of the GNP is devoted to health care, but the more money expended, the unhealthier our people are.

When you eat three fatty meals a day, there's a continuous sludging resulting in poor oxygen and other nutrients. Symptoms like leg pains, walking, strokes, fatigue, decreased endurance, chest pains, loss of hearing, loss of balance, and reduced lung function is the result ("McDougall Plan").

Tumor growth is retarded by a low fat diet (McDougall).

Dr. William Adler (at the National Institute on Aging, Baltimore) says that what you eat is exceedingly important to your immune system. Zinc fortifies. We should recognize a deficiency in the elderly. Zinc foods, cheese, liver, meat, poultry, and nuts.

There are many wonder foods we have to choose from:

Beans have carbohydrates, calcium, and Vitamin B.
They have high quality protein.
Low in fat
Have fiber and important minerals.

Fatty fish, herring, mackerel are good for triglycerides.

Also 1/4 gram capsule of B3 taken daily (Orthomolecular Nutrition).

Foods for defense: fish, non-fatty cheese, raw fruit and vegetables, yogurt, low fat, low salt (restrict intake).

For defense against cancer: broccoli, brussel sprouts, cabbage, cauliflower.

Nucleic acid for the cells: sardines, salmon.

Cayenne pepper is a digestive aid. It calls to arms all secreting organs. Great for seniors in the morning wake-up drink.

Apple cider vinegar taken with meals supplements hydrochloric acid and is therefore an aid to digestion.

Vinegar, butternuts, meat, eggs, grains, liver, seafood.

"If the power to digest is not increased, all attempts to build will be useless" (Shelton).

It is difficult to get a benefit from nutrients unless you're exercising.

Dr. Walker says that the most natural salt in celery juice is one of the most valuable for people who have used concentrated sugar and starches all their lives. (That's all of us!)

Wheat germ has 76 times more niacin than enriched white flour.

More than three times the riboflavin (for eyes)
Eight times more thiamin.
Three times more protein.
Four times more iron.
Eight times more potassium.
Store wheat germ in the freezer.

B12 alleviates disorientation, fatigue, confusion:

eggs, liver, beef, dairy.

Joke: One man ate all health foods, died, and went to heaven. There he was served carrots and celery sticks, but noticed down there was much feasting, so he complained to St. Peter.

"How come I don't get decent food up here?" St. Peter answered, "Up here it doesn't pay to cook for two."

Some of my favorite recipes:

Instant Soup:

1/2 can chicken broth (do not add water)
1 clove chopped garlic
1/2 cup chick peas, cooked
1/3 cup chopped parsley or bean sprouts

Add all ingredients to soup when it comes to a boil.

Pita Surprise:

Fill toasted whole wheat pita bread with:

1 clove chopped garlic
1/8 cup chopped parsley
1/8 cup chopped sprouts
tomato
avocado
cucumber
3 or 4 black dried black olives cut up
few pieces herring
chopped onion
2/3 tablespoons apple cider vinegar

Oatmeal Supreme:

To my breakfast oat bran, I add the following:

1 tablespoon rice polish
1 tablespoon corn flour with lysine

My peanut butter recipe is in the chapter on aging.

And don't forget carrot juice, two or three sardine meals a week, one salmon meal a week, and one liver meal a week.

Also, remember cayenne pepper starts the juices flowing, so why shouldn't we—

FEEL GOOD!

CHAPTER THIRTY-SEVEN

INTERESTING FACTS

Cream has Vitamin A, calcium, magnesium, and riboflavin.

Apple cider vinegar combines with alkaline elements and minerals to produce energy (Walker).

There are carcinogens in water (Dr. Oliver Alabaster, "What You Can Do To Prevent Cancer").

Less protein reduces the risk of cancer (Dr. Alabaster).

Yucca tablets seem to have a role in reducing cholesterol and triglyceride levels in the blood and gives relief from arthritis (Winters).

Chewing a small piece of garlic purifies the teeth, gums, tongue, and throat, and rids intestines of parasites and mucus all the way down to the colon (Winters).

Cleansing the bowel cures many diseases (Winters).

Bran can only propel the new daily fecal matter through the already clogged colon (Winters).

A coffee enema detoxifies the liver.

A coffee enema stimulates the bowel walls.

A coffee enema relieves headache (Winters).

Potassium foods:

> lean meat, horseradish, whole grains, vegetables, legumes, bananas, sunflower seeds.

Excessive crying or itching around eyes, nose, ears, indicates outside irritants.

Vitamin C starts metabolism and keeps joints flexible—also improves immunity in elderly.

Iron foods:

> Organ meats, egg yolk, fish, oysters, whole grains, beans, green vegetables, beef, chicken, fish, liver, beets.

> Vitamin C with these doubles the amount of iron absorbed.

Zinc, cheese, liver, meat, poultry, nuts (this stimulates smell and taste).

Anti-radiation bath:

> 1 lb pure salt, not iodized
> 1 lb baking soda

> Hot bath twice a week for one month.

For pain:

> Wrap rubber bands around tips of fingers.
> Squeeze comb in palm of hand, reaching all areas.
> Apply clothespin to areas on hands.

Iron helps ward off infections.

It is believed iron carries oxygen to the cells:

> in meat, liver, eggs, leafy green vegetables.

Garlic makes red blood corpuscles. Molasses, beans, peas are all good blood builders. Also red meat and beets.

Honey contains important elements for making good blood.

Chick peas are loaded with nutrients. Their yield of protein per cultivated acre is higher than any other leguminous grain with the exception of peanuts. They have calcium, iron, and are a cancer inhibitor.

Sesame seeds are high in protein and have a unique amino acid composition. They contain methionine and tryptophan. Eat halvah. Jason Winters says that in Eastern countries it was believed halvah made women sexy.

Lecithin is a brain food. Take it when tired, fatigued. Also fish, avocado, dried olives, and egg yolks (Jensen).

Calcium in:

> dark green vegetables, dairy, meat, sardines, apricots, horseradish, salmon, seafood.

Sulphur (for pituitary gland) in:

> garlic, onions, radish, cayenne pepper.

Potassium in:

> lean meat, whole grains, vegetables, legumes, sunflower seeds, bananas.

For stress, pantothenic acid foods:

> organ meats, yeast, eggs, sweet potatoes, whole grains, salmon.

Chlorophyll for digestion.

Bee pollen aids the undigested food in the body (one of the culprits for forming poisons).

Polyunsaturated fat helps lower cholesterol in blood whenever used as a substitute in cooking. Also, nuts and seeds.

Kelp for energy--several tablets a day.

An energy pick up: Lemon in water with a dash of cayenne pepper. Or grape juice with a dash of cayenne (especially for seniors).

Carbohydrate intake should be raised from 45% of the diet to 70%. (This helps you sleep better, too.)

Toxins come from foods not properly digested and assimilated, as cooked, fried, processed, barbecued, and sauteed.

For stimulating the appetite:

> onions, paprika, oregano, lemon, dill weed, ginger, allspice, cinnamon, cheese.

Magnesium:

> buckwheat flour, black-eye peas, nuts, tofu, kidney beans, limas, bananas, shredded wheat.

CHAPTER THIRTY-EIGHT

THE END

When we start life, we're all given a deposit in the bank. We then draw on this deposit. We can use it wisely or squander it, but we can't add to it. We can't put anything into the account.

So it is how we spend it that determines our life span. We have the opportunity to slow down the withdrawals and thus make the account last longer.

By doing this, we can feel good, and even feel young, into our 70's and 80's.

Eubie Blake, the black songwriter approaching his 100th birthday, said, "If I knew I was gonna live this long, I would have taken better care of myself."

So we can still feel good, and let's all sing (to the tune of "Three Coins in the Fountain")—

Make it last, make it last, make it last!

The best doctors in the world are:

Dr. Diet,

Dr. Quiet, and

Dr. Merryman

(Jonathan Swift, "Polite Conversation")

Selye, Hans, _Modern Maturity_, Nov, 1987.

Shelton, Herbert M., _Hygienic Review._

Shulman, Julius, _Cataracts_, Simon & Shuster, 1984.

Siegel, Bernard S., _Love, Medicine and Miracles_, Harper & Row, 1986.

Tilden, John H., _Toxemia, The Basic Cause of Disease_, Natural Hygiene Press.

Trattler, Ross, _Better Health Through Natural Healing_, McGraw Hill Book Co., NY.

Walker, Norman W., _Fresh Vegetable & Fruit Juices_, Norwalk Press, Phoenix, AZ, 1936.

Winters, Jason, _In Search of The Perfect Cleanse_, Vinton Publishing Co.

INDEX

BIBLIOGRAPHY

Asai, Nazuhiko, Miracle Cure—Organic Germanium, Japan Publications, USA.

Alabaster, Oliver, Preventing Cancer, Norton Publishers.

Berkson, Devaki, The Foot Book, Barnes & Noble.

Berkson & Tuchak, Zone Therapy, Pinnacle Books, Inc.

Carter, Mildred, Helping Yourself With Foot Reflexology and Hand Reflexology, The Key to Perfect Health, Parker Publishers, W. Nyack, NY.

Diamond, H & M, Fit for Life, Warner Books.

Ecker & Bramesco, Radiation, Vintage Books.

Frank, Benjamin S., The No Aging Diet, Dial Press, 1976.

Future Youth, Prevention, Rodale Press.

Hanna, Thomas, The Body of Life, Knopf, 1980.

Hoffer & Walker, Orthomolecular Nutrition, Keats Publishing, Inc., New Canaan, CT.

Hoopes, A & T, Eye Power, Alfred A. Knopf, NY.

Jarvis, D.C., Folk Medicine, Henry Holt & Co., Greenwich, CT.

Jensen, Bernard, Nature Has a Remedy, Escondido, CA.

Hafen & Frandsen, From Acupuncture to Yoga, Prentice Hall, Englewood Cliffs, NJ.

Kamen, B & S, *In Pursuit of Youth*, Dodd Mead & Co., NY.

Kenyon, Keith, *Do It Yourself Acupuncture Without Needles*, Arco Publishers, NY.

Kugler, Hans, *The Disease of Aging*, Keats Publishing Co., New Canaan, CT.

Kushner, Harold, *When All You Ever Wanted Wasn't Enough*, Pocket Books.

Levenson, Frederick B., *Causes & Prevention of Cancer*, Stein & Day, 1984.

Mann, Felix, *Acupuncture, The Ancient Art of Healing and How it Works Scientifically*, Vintage Books, Division of Random House, NY.

McDougall & McDougall, *The McDougall Plan*, New Century, Publishers.

Peale, Norman Vincent, *The Power of Positive Thinking*, Prentice Hall, Publishers.

Pelletier, Kenneth R., *Mind as Healer—Mind as Slayer*, Dell Publishing Co., NY, 1977.

Petrek, Jeanne A., *A Woman's Guide to the Prevention, Detection, and Treatment of Cancer*, MacMillen Publishing Co., NY.

Pizer, Hank, *Guide to New Medicine*.

Randolph & Moss, *Alternative Approach to Allergies*, Bantam Publishers, 1982.

Robertson, Donald S. & Carol P., *The Snowbird Diet*, Warner Books.

Schneider, Robert G., *Cancer Prevention Made Easy*, Prentice Hall, Englewood, NJ.